52
Devotions
for
CHURCH
LEADERS

52
Devotions
for
CHURCH
LEADERS

Robert H. Ramey, Jr.

Chalice Press
St. Louis, Missouri

All scripture quotations, unless otherwise indicated, are from the *New Revised Standard Version Bible,* copyright 1989, Division of Christian Education of the National Council of the Churches of Christ in the USA. Used by permission.

Reprinted by permission of Simon & Schuster, from *The New Testament in Modern English,* revised edition, translated by J. B. Phillips. © 1958, 1960, 1972 by J. B. Phillips.

Cover design: Elizabeth Wright
Interior design: Elizabeth Wright

This book is printed on acid-free, recycled paper.

Visit Chalice Press on the World Wide Web at
www.chalicepress.com

10 9 8 7 6 5 4 3 2 1   98 99 00 01 02 03

Library of Congress Cataloging–in–Publication Data

Ramey, Robert H. (Robert Homer)
    52 devotions for church leaders / by Robert H. Ramey, Jr.
       p.   cm.
    Includes bibliographical references.
    ISBN 0-8272-1023-X
    1. Christian leadership–Prayer–books and devotions—English.
I. Title. II. Title: Fifty two devotions for church leaders.
BV652.1.R35 1999
242'.69 — dc21   98-43549
                                                         CIP

Printed in the United States of America

to
Jane Robbins Ramey
1930–1983
who
embodied
Christian leadership,
the purpose
of this book.

Contents

Introduction

For many years I have reflected on church leadership, first as a pastor, then as a professor. Leadership is a fascinating and absorbing subject, but the more I study it, the more complicated it becomes. Still, certain abiding truths have emerged from my studies over the years, and I would like to share them with you in devotional form. By no means are most of these insights original—I have learned from many teachers and students.

I have arranged these insights to include the foundations, characteristics, and skills of Christian leadership, as well as its varied problems. I have written these devotionals specifically for church boards, staffs, and committees to use in their meetings. I hope you will share one at every meeting. If time permits, you can discuss the devotional for a few minutes, employing the questions provided in the Appendix. Pick and choose devotionals from each section, if you wish—they are not necessarily sequential.

More specifically, church boards may read one of the devotionals each time they meet. If they choose, they can alternate and select one from a different section. Boards that meet monthly will have enough material to cover at least four years of meetings.

Church staffs can work with one of the devotionals weekly when they meet. They will have sufficient material for a year of staff meetings.

Church committees and other groups can simply use the book as needed. All who chair a committee may wish a copy.

Also, newly installed members of boards, staffs, or committees can read the book for fifty-two days following their installation to office. Pastors, especially, may want to follow this plan when moving to a new pastorate.

However you use the material, may these brief pages help you become a more faithful and effective Christian leader. That is my greatest hope.

Robert H. Ramey, Jr.
March 1998

PART 1

Foundations
of Christian
Leadership

Called by God

> "Now the LORD said to Abram, 'Go from your country and your kindred and your father's house to the land that I will show you'" (Gen. 12:1). *Read Genesis 12:1–9.*

God called Abraham—then known as Abram—to go from his country and his people to a new land. God also promised him not only land, but also descendants, and a blessing. And Abraham obeyed God's call, packed up his family and possessions, and headed out, not knowing where they would go. What an improbable but incredible story!

God also has called *you* personally in several ways. God called you to be a disciple of Jesus Christ. God also called you to your job in the world. Whether you are a student, homemaker, computer programmer, CEO, or salesperson, God called you. And God further called you to serve in the church as a pastor, elder, deacon, council member, teacher, musician, or rank-and-file member.

Our awesome God works mysteriously "his wonders to perform." As we meditate upon God, or God's work of creation or redemption, or God's law, we hear God calling us. As we reflect on God's grace and our need, we hear God calling. As we consider the world's cries for help and our ability to respond, we hear God calling. *In the innermost recesses of our hearts we hear God calling.* God calls us personally.

It's crucial to understand that *you* have to decide every facet of your call. Oh, I know. Sometimes people say, "This is what you ought to do." Do they ever really know what you ought to do? Do they know exactly what it's like to be you, to feel as you feel, to think as you think? And since when should anyone else take responsibility for your life? Of course, it's important to listen to the shared wisdom of others—they can help us immensely. Yet they cannot and should not make our decisions for us.

So, God calls you personally as God called Abraham long ago. In that respect you travel alone. As you may have heard, "No one can hitchhike on another's spiritual journey!"[1] Sure, we need companions along the way, as did Abraham. And we in the church of today belong to a community of faith.

But others cannot live our lives. My call and your call are personal. And we can thank God for that. Does it not show how much God values and respects each one of us?

Chosen to Serve

"You did not choose me but I chose you. And I ap-
pointed you to go and bear fruit..." (John 15:16a). *Read
John 15:12–17.*

How did you begin to serve the church? I am inviting
you to retrace your steps to your present position
whether you are a minister, board member, or other leader.

Did your journey not begin when you heard Jesus'
words, "You did not choose me but I chose you"? You
realized that you had been called to follow Jesus, to be his
disciple.

Then did you have a desire to serve Jesus in a particular
way? Perhaps you wanted to become a minister or to serve
the church as a leader, so you began to pray toward that
end. In secret you nurtured your emerging call.

Or maybe someone in your church came to you one
day and said, "Have you ever thought about becoming a
minister?" or, "We would like for you to consider serving as
a board member," or, "Would you think about using your
gift of leadership to chair the worship committee?" Awed
and humbled by the gifts they saw in you, you prayed for
God to guide you further.

But then the church participated more directly in your
call. If a minister, the church guided you in your prepara-
tion for ministry. If a board member, the church trained
you for your job. If a committee chair, the church prepared

you to take over the reins of leading the committee. But in every case the church was vitally involved in your call to service. The position you took was far more than an *inner* call; an *outer* call from the church was also necessary. You did not suddenly appear in church one day and announce that you were going to assume a certain leadership position.

Chosen originally by Jesus to follow him, you as a leader have also been chosen by the church. Don't take that lightly, even though you know how flawed you are. Again and again persons have said to me, "I am not worthy. I've got a lot of faults." To which I reply, "So do I. We were not called because we are perfect, but because Christ and his people want us to serve. Remember this: Your fellow Christians see in you a person who has the qualities they want in a leader." That's humbling, but also empowering. To think that God uses weak, earthen vessels like us to perform Christian service!

Rooted and Built Up in Christ

"As you therefore have received Christ Jesus the Lord, continue to live your lives in him, rooted and built up in him and established in the faith..." (Col. 2:6, 7). *Read Colossians 2:6–19.*

Is there really any other place for Christian leaders to ground their work except in Christ Jesus? Surely not, yet we are tempted to look elsewhere for our grounding. Are we not tossed to and fro by everything from consumerism to New Age teaching, from permissive morality to strident nationalism?

So it has been for a long time now, ever since Paul wrote to an imperiled little band of Christians in Colossae. Their environment tended to corrupt the pure gospel Epaphras taught them as he had learned it from Paul. Colossian Christians, for example, were embracing strange teachings, including certain ascetic practices. They might even have forbidden marriage, saying, "Do not touch" (Col. 2:21b). Even more, gnostic teaching was infiltrating the community. Gnostics taught that human beings leave the material world behind and climb a spiritual ladder if they want to make contact with God. Somewhat similarly, in 1997 the Heaven's Gate suicide cult in Rancho Santa Fe, California, decided to leave their "human containers" behind when they poisoned themselves, hoping to go to the Father's kingdom.

As for Christ, the false teachers in Colossae relegated him to a *high*, though not *supreme* place. Perhaps the Colossians thought the gospel they had learned was too simple and needed asceticism and gnosticism to make it better. Yet Paul would have none of it. "Hold fast to the faith Epaphras taught you," he said. "Continue to live in Christ, relying on him as your daily companion."

That's timely advice for Christian leaders today. We need no modern "add-ons" like New Age teaching, or the occult, or the ascetic to make our faith more complete. For the tradition we have received has stood the test of time and resisted every assault upon its integrity. Now, Christians are not opposed to new truth. In fact, Jesus said, "When the Spirit of truth comes, he will guide you into all the truth…" (John 16:13a). Even so, Jesus added, "He will glorify *me*, because he will take what is *mine* and declare it to you" (John 16:14, italics mine).

Let's build our work together on Christ, the sure foundation, the source of truth. Any other foundation will eventually collapse.

Empowered by the Spirit

"Therefore, friends, select from among yourselves seven men of good standing, full of the Spirit..."(Acts 6:3). *Read Acts 6:1–6.*

S trange, isn't it, how we sometimes select people to serve on our church boards, staffs, and committees? If they are *active*, or have *stature* in the community, or are *popular*, or are *go-getters*, we pick them. Of course, each of these qualities can help any leader. But when selecting leaders, are we not missing some key ingredients for faithful and effective leaders?

When the Twelve felt burdened by serving meals, they asked the infant Christian community to select seven men to take their place while they prayed and preached. And what were the criteria for their "search committee" to follow? The apostles told them to select seven men "of good standing, *full of the Spirit* and of wisdom..." (Acts 6:3, italics mine). They chose Stephen, "a man *full of faith and the Holy Spirit*..." (Acts 6:5b, italics mine). One emerging criterion for leadership was to be full of the Spirit.

Stephen evidently possessed the required criteria, including being full of the Holy Spirit. Not just the spirit of good will, not just the spirit of friendliness, and not just community spirit, but the *Holy* Spirit. A leader could possess all those other spirits, yet not be full of the Holy Spirit. And a crucial dynamic would be missing.

Oh, I know, we can keep the lights burning in our churches with these other spirits, but we lack real power. When leaders are empowered by the Holy Spirit, they look different, they act differently. They do what Christ wants, not what culture dictates. *In a word, they live and make decisions in the power of the Spirit.*

No wonder that "Stephen, full of grace and power, did great wonders and signs among the people" (Acts 6:8). Also, just before his witness cost him his life we read: "But *filled with the Holy Spirit*, he gazed into heaven and saw the glory of God and Jesus standing at the right hand of God" (Acts 7:55, italics mine). Amazing! Stephen began his ministry full of the Holy Spirit; he ended it the same way.

Not that any of us modern leaders long for martyrdom, but shouldn't we also tap into the power that changed the world, *the power of the Holy Spirit?*

Connected with the Body of Christ

> "For as in one body we have many members, and not all the members have the same function, so we, who are many, are one body in Christ, and individually we are members of one another. We have gifts that differ according to the grace given to us…" (Rom. 12:4–6a). *Read Romans 12:3–9.*

We Americans are rugged individualists, right? Well, let's see.

I admire the frontier spirit that left such a legacy in our history. At times our ancestors confronted more obstacles in a week than we have to face in a year. And they often had no one else to depend on; it was either sink or swim.

Also, I respect CEOs who sometimes have to make quick, tough, lonely decisions. To some extent are they not the modern counterpart of people on the frontier? So we do have a history of rugged individualism in this nation.

Thus it's hard for us to change gears and understand what it means to belong to a *body*. Yet when we became Christians we also became members of the church, Christ's body. *In other words, we were baptized into Christ and into his body.* And that's radically different from seeing ourselves as rugged individualists upon whom rests our well-being and security.

Now we see that we belong to Christ and his body, not to ourselves. Of course we have different functions in the body. I am a minister, while you may be a music director. But though we possess different gifts, we all use them for the common good, for the community. We stop thinking that we, individually, must do it all and don't need anyone, anywhere, any time. Rather, I use my gifts for the community, and you contribute yours. I preach, for example, and you sing. (You surely don't want *me* to sing—I can only make a "joyful noise!") Yet both music and preaching are essential gifts in every church.

Christ's work, then, doesn't depend on us alone. Is not Christ the head of the church? And are we not "members of one another"? But we do have functions to fulfill and gifts to use for the community. So, as Paul says here, the leader should be diligent in using those gifts. (See Rom. 12:8.)

Enriched by Fellowship

> "We declare to you what we have seen and heard so that you also may have fellowship with us; and truly our fellowship is with the Father and with his Son Jesus Christ" (1 John 1:3). *Read 1 John 1:1–10.*

Don't most of us long for fellowship? for companionship with people who help us to be ourselves? for friendship with others who share our core values? for togetherness with persons who help us celebrate the sheer joy of living?

Some of us not only long for fellowship, but thrive on it. We delight in people so much that we can hardly stand to be alone. Others, however, are quieter, preferring only occasional forays into the world of human companionship. Either way, all of us must find it or live more and more isolated from people.

Do not church leaders also need fellowship to carry out their jobs? So we join staff members at a coffee break, or play softball at a board retreat, or have a picnic with the choir. Such occasions help us relax and enjoy one another.

Beneath all church fellowship lies a deeper reality: our faith. Our fellowship is "with the Father and with his Son Jesus Christ." *That* fellowship makes possible our deep friendship with one another. *Divine* fellowship enriches *human* fellowship. They are interrelated, of course, for human fellowship may initiate our relationship with God.

Can we be devoted and competent leaders without fellowship? Hardly, though I've seen many church leaders try. They are either too busy or too serious about their work. But God did not intend for us to live alone. God has provided a way for us to overcome our isolation and loneliness and to find the friendship we need. If we truly have fellowship "with the Father and with his Son Jesus Christ," we will also have fellowship with one another. And as we do so, we may discover that our relationship with God is enriched.

> Blest be the tie that binds
> Our hearts in Christian love.
> The fellowship of kindred minds
> Is like to that above.[2]

Indeed it is!

Surrounded by Witnesses

"Therefore, since we are surrounded by so great a cloud of witnesses, let us also lay aside every weight and the sin that clings so closely..." (Heb. 12:1). *Read Hebrews 12:1–11.*

To lead a church is often lonely. We never know whether the plans we make now will work out. And we cannot prove scientifically that the faith we proclaim is even valid. The world may scoff at core ideas of faith like Christ's saving death on the cross and his resurrection. Thus exercising *Christian* leadership can be daunting for even the most courageous among us.

Though lonely, we are not really alone, unless we are foolish. God has not left us without witnesses to God's love and power. Abraham and Sarah, Moses, Rahab, Gideon— on and on goes the list in Hebrews of those who served as witnesses to the reality of God. They did not even receive what God had promised, but they lived by faith in God's promises.

And how those faithful witnesses strengthen us on lonely days when we become discouraged! More than mere spectators of our struggles, they also serve as witnesses to a faithful God who keeps promises. Looking at their strong witness helps us stand firm in our faith when our knees tremble and our hearts grow faint. Moreover, their strong witness helps us lay aside every sin and "run with perseverance the race that is set before us..." (Heb. 12:1b).

So on troubling days, when storm clouds gather ominously, remember that great cloud of witnesses from the roll call of faith in Hebrews. But don't stop there. Look at the witnesses in your own denomination whether Martin Luther, John Calvin, John Wesley, Thomas Cranmer, Alexander Campbell, or Roger Williams. Look at the heroes and heroines of the Roman Catholic Church, whether Teresa of Avila, Francis of Assisi, or Teresa of Calcutta. All of them witnessed to a faithful God.

Also look to Jesus, "the pioneer and perfecter of our faith..." (Heb. 12:2). By faith he trusted God even though he was nailed to a cross. Jesus is the supreme witness to a faithful God, for God raised him from the dead.

Alone, yet not alone, we put our hands to the plow—or computer—once more. And surrounded by so great a cloud of witnesses—and looking to Jesus—we will not fail.

Devoted to Prayer

"Therefore, friends, select...seven men of good standing, full of the Spirit and of wisdom...while we, for our part, will devote ourselves to prayer and serving the word" (Acts 6:3,4). *Read Acts 6:1–4.*

How often do you pray in your church meetings? And when do you pray? Unless you are different from most churches you probably engage in "bookend prayers." You open your meetings with prayer and close them with prayer. In between those prayers you conduct business. But does not prayer sometimes become a mechanical custom to follow?

Not so with the early church! The Twelve wanted the Christian community to select seven men to serve tables so that they could devote themselves to prayer and serving the word. Praying was an integral part of their job description, not a routine practice.

A long, conflicted board meeting was trying my patience and causing knots in my stomach. Right in the middle of our muddle, an elder said, "I think we ought to stop and have prayer. We're going in the wrong direction here." I'll admit I was irritated. "He's uncomfortable with the debate so he's attempting to divert us," I reflected. But how could I oppose prayer? As we prayed, I began to calm down. We then carefully devised a plan of action to lead us toward resolving our conflict. And in time we resolved it.

With the apostles, I now clearly see that we, too, need to devote ourselves to prayer. Do we think we can govern our little church domains without praying often and sincerely? Do we know something that the apostles didn't know? Hardly. They *knew* what we must *learn*: To lead well we must offer ourselves to God in prayer. Only as we do so can we unlock the tremendous power that flows from a dynamic relationship with God. When we pray, we receive insights we had not seen before. And we see one another as children of God, who are our friends in Christ, searching for God's will in whatever we do.

Pray, therefore, at the beginning of a meeting. Then appoint persons to pray silently, on a rotating basis, for fifteen minutes at a time during the meeting. And when you get stuck, as you most certainly will, stop and pray about it as a group.

One other idea: Begin to pray for the next meeting long before it starts!

Guided by Scripture

"All scripture is inspired by God and is useful for teaching, for reproof, for correction, and for training in righteousness..." (2 Tim. 3:16). *Read 2 Timothy 3:10–17.*

Here we are again, reading a passage of scripture and focusing on yet another text. We ordinarily engage in this practice in our church meetings. Often we base our services of worship on scripture from the call to worship to the benediction. When we want to know the will of God, we search the Bible for clues to God's will. Is not scripture indeed powerful and helpful for living the Christian life? And leaders, of all people, need to be guided by it.

As we ponder this text, we cannot be as clear as we would like. For example, does "all scripture" include the New Testament as well as the Old? Scholars differ. Does "inspired by God" mean that God dictated every word and concept, including scientific viewpoints? How you answer these questions depends upon your own perspective and denomination. More important here is for us to see that leaders in the church are to be guided by scripture. Have we not found it "useful for teaching, for reproof, for correction, and for training in righteousness"?

But so much for the principle—what about our practice? Are we conscientiously studying scripture so that it can be useful? Scripture can hardly be a valuable authority for us if our Bibles are gathering dust!

No matter how guilty we may feel about our practice, our situation is by no means hopeless. You can start by reading some scripture everyday. Read it privately, read it in a group. Gradually you will read through an entire book, even a testament. Apply what you read to your own life. Brood over its meaning. And do you know what will happen? As you steep yourself in God's Word, you will find it guiding you more and more. You will use scripture in leading the church, as well as in growing in grace. You will discover that "the sacred writings...instruct you for salvation through faith in Christ Jesus" (2 Tim. 3:15).

Strange, isn't it, that we neglect to read and study the Bible, the Church's book? But you can begin again. Without wallowing in guilt, simply start today.

Motivated by Love

"...you shall love the Lord your God with all your heart, and with all your soul, and with all your mind, and with all your strength. The second is this, 'You shall love your neighbor as yourself'" (Mark 12:30). *Read Mark 12: 28–34.*

An old song asks, "What's it all about, Alfie?" In other words, what is the meaning and purpose of life? A lot of people would like to know! In a recent poll of the spiritual needs of Americans, 70 percent said their number one need was to find meaning and purpose in life.

A scribe—a teacher of the law—asked Jesus one day which commandment was the first of all. Jesus replied, drawing upon the "Shema" in Deuteronomy 6 and reiterating that to love God with your whole being is the greatest commandment. He went on to add that the second commandment is to love your neighbor as yourself.

In a nutshell Jesus identified the gospel's answer to the question put to Alfie, "What's it all about?" Love God with your whole being and your neighbor as yourself, and your life will have meaning and purpose. Every single time.

I've taken three paragraphs to specify that church leaders need to love God and neighbor. You may have already assumed as much.

But I want to stress the obvious. *If we are leaders in Christ's church in any capacity, we have to be growing in our love for God and neighbor.*

Now we wouldn't lay this requirement upon a leader in business or industry. (Even if we expected it!) But loving God and neighbor is part of the foundation for any Christian leader. The purpose of the church and its ministry, H. Richard Niebuhr contended, is "the increase of love of God and neighbor."[3] This is the only way members will find meaning and purpose in their lives. And leaders must show them the way. They can't expect others to follow a road they haven't traveled themselves.

So do a spiritual audit. Ask yourself, "Am I growing in my love for God with all my heart, soul, mind, and strength? Do I love my neighbor as I love myself?"

Of course, you fall short of perfection, but are you at least *growing* in your love for God and neighbor? If not, this text may drive you to your knees in prayer. But what better place to begin than to pray that God will help you become more loving as you seek to lead others to love.

Focused on the Kingdom of God

"But strive first for the kingdom of God and his righteousness, and all these things will be given to you as well" (Matt. 6:33). *Read Matthew 6:25–34.*

Recently I tried to identify the most faithful and effective Christian leaders I had ever known. Several people came to mind at once. Then I asked myself, "What were they like? What distinguished them from everyone else?" In each case I concluded that they put the kingdom of God *first* in their lives. Not second or third or fourth behind job or nation or even family, but first. Now, they all did their jobs well, loved their nation, and cherished their families, but they were focused on the kingdom of God. And therein lay the secret of their amazing effectiveness and influence in every area of their lives.

Such leaders knew that God's rule or reign was at the epicenter of the message and ministry of Jesus. Moreover, Jesus himself, as crucified and risen Lord and Savior, was at the epicenter of the kingdom. Thus the kingdom of God became the kingdom of Christ. To say that these leaders put the kingdom first meant that they focused on Christ. He was at the epicenter of their lives.

Yet the temptation before all leaders—and Christians as well—is to fall prey to the "what if" syndrome. What if all these plans we're making fall flat? What if we don't have enough money to finance our hopes and dreams? What if we can't enlist enough volunteers to do the job? Do we not almost "what if" ourselves to death?

Jesus said such worry is fruitless. Clothes, food, drink—the necessities of life—preoccupy us constantly. But according to Jesus, God knows our basic needs and will supply them. God also cares about all of our other worries, certainly these "what if" thoughts that plague us in church work.

Yes, God cares about us and provides for our needs. But Jesus teaches us to strive for the kingdom of God first. Let concern for the reign of God be at the heart of every dream we have, every decision we make, every conflict we seek to resolve.

A worry-wart like me needs to remember Jesus' counsel. For if there's a way to imagine that something will go wrong, I can usually think of it! Then I have to stop and reflect on the most faithful and effective leaders I have known. Their memory steadies me and helps me focus once again. Maybe this exercise will help you, too.

Endowed with Faith

"...for he was a good man, full of the Holy Spirit and of faith" (Acts 11:24). *Read Acts 11:19–26.*

When the twelve apostles were casting about for seven men to wait on tables, they chose Stephen first of all. Stephen was *full of faith.* Later in the book of Acts, it was also said about Barnabas that "he was a good man, full of the Holy Spirit and *of faith*" (Acts 11:24, italics mine). Paul himself said, "And the life I now live in the flesh I live *by faith* in the Son of God, who loved me and gave himself for me" (Gal. 2:20). Are we on to something here? Let's see.

Apparently, one of the defining characteristics of early Christian leaders was their faith in the Son of God, who loved them and gave himself for them. Faith in Jesus as Lord, who ushered in the reign of God and at whose name "every knee should bend" (Phil. 2:10). Faith in Jesus as Savior, who came to seek and to save the lost. Thus can't we conclude that faith in Jesus Christ was an indispensable quality of Christian leadership? It was, and it still is!

Why is it so essential for church leaders to have faith in Jesus Christ? Isn't it enough for them to be successful in business? to be leaders in the community? to possess energy and imagination? Unfortunately, the answer is No. *The perspective that faith in Jesus Christ gives is an absolute requirement for Christian leaders.*

Faith in Jesus Christ informs the *purpose of your work.* You will seek "the mind of Christ" in all that you do.

Faith in Jesus Christ informs *how you spend the church's money.* If a wealthy member dies and leaves the church $100,000 in her will, you will use that money to best serve Jesus Christ and "the least of these" for whom he died.

Faith in Jesus Christ informs *the spirit in which you serve.* You will not use your leadership position to lord it over others, but to serve as did Jesus who "came not to be served but to serve…" (Mark 10:45).

Faith in Jesus Christ informs *how you look at culture.* Instead of automatically embracing whatever is new and trendy, you will ask, "How does this fit with the gospel?"

So add faith in Jesus Christ to the essential qualities for Christian leaders. May all of your church leaders be endowed with such faith.

Urged On by Christ's Love

"For the love of Christ urges us on, because we are convinced that one has died for all; therefore all have died" (2 Cor. 5:14). *Read 2 Corinthians 5:11–15.*

Church work, as fulfilling as it often is, can puzzle, discourage, and exhaust the best of us. Some of you may say, "That's the understatement of the year." Others who are new in the work of the church may not understand my statement at all. You haven't yet experienced the truth of a late medieval manuscript that said: "The church is something like Noah's ark. If it weren't for the storm outside, you couldn't stand the smell inside."[4]

But why even make the point? Because any who would lead the church must be firmly grounded in the love of Christ. Paul probably refers here to Christ's love for us, not our love for Christ. *That love urges us on when the going gets tough.* It's love that is willing to be vulnerable. In the person of Christ, it took hostility in the form of taunts and jeers. It absorbed spears and nails. And it even died forgiving those who inflicted the pain! Only a love like that can be strong enough to help us when we face discouragement and pain.

And those difficult days inevitably come. I just talked with a friend who has been bitterly hurt by the church. She will rise again to serve the church and take on the world. But how? Because the love of Christ urges her on. She knows it's a love that will never let her go.

Thus we rest our leadership upon the love of Christ. Any other footing is likely to fail us when life crashes in upon us.

Can money provide staying power?

Can popularity keep us steady?

Can a good track record of service anchor us?

All such ballast is too weak for dark and difficult days.

Only one rock will keep us secure: the love of Christ.

So back to the tasks that Christ calls us to perform.

Back to the burdens he wants us to bear.

Back to the wrongs we must right.

For the love of Christ urges us on.

Characteristics of Christian Leaders

Doers of the Word

"But be doers of the word, and not merely hearers who deceive themselves" (James 1:22). *Read James 1:22–27.*

Does anything hurt the cause of Christ more than hypocrisy? It's unlikely. Critics of the Christian faith constantly taunt us, saying, "We'll take more interest in your faith when we see a living, breathing Christian walking around!" That hurts.

Perhaps nowhere do we need a Christian example more than in church leadership positions. Thus we say to our leaders, "Practice what you preach. Walk the talk. Demonstrate the gospel in your life." Then the coup de grâce from James: "Be doers of the word, and not merely hearers who deceive themselves."

Of course, God calls *all* Christians to be doers of the word. We misunderstand the faith if we establish two classes of Christians—one for leaders, the other for members. When I was a pastor, few things bothered me more than hearing members say they thought God required a higher standard for me than for them. I felt like saying to them, "That's a cop-out. You're rationalizing your own failure to be more faithful Christians." To one and all the gospel says, "Be holy. Let your entire life breathe the vitality of Christ."

And yet, I'll admit that when leaders are merely hearers of the word it seems to be especially harmful. It turns off people outside the church; it also turns off people inside the church who look to leaders for direction. *They want to see the fruit of the Spirit in us.* And "the fruit of the Spirit is love, joy, peace, patience, kindness, generosity, faithfulness, gentleness, and self-control" (Gal. 5:22).

When I read that list, I realize how far I fall short. It probably makes you wince, too. But God doesn't want us to flounder in a sea of guilt. Doesn't God want us to build on the foundations that produce the fruit of the Spirit? So ground your life in Jesus Christ. Confess your sins and receive forgiveness. Live by the power of the Spirit. And practice the disciplines God has given us for growth.

Even so, our sin will always block us from perfectly doing everything we hear in the gospel. But—thanks be to God—we are sinners saved by grace and called to manifest the fruit of the Spirit. In God's grace lies our hope.

Forgive Each Other!

"Bear with one another and, if anyone has a complaint against another, forgive each other; just as the Lord has forgiven you, so you also must forgive" (Col. 3:13). *Read Colossians 3:12–17.*

Frankly, I am puzzled about where to lodge forgiveness in this book. Is it a foundation of leadership? a skill? a quality? Or all of the above? Perhaps the latter, and more.

Surely, being able to forgive is a must for Christian leaders. To confess our sins and be forgiven is the beginning point for our spiritual journey. Without this substructure, our work as leaders in Christ's church will always be lacking. For we constantly need to forgive *each other* as Christ has forgiven *us*. Unless we understand the power of forgiveness in *our* lives, we can hardly reach out to others in Christ's name and say, "I forgive *you*."

Regardless of your position in the church, the day will come when you need to be forgiven. You will blow up in a meeting and say things you don't mean. Or you will suddenly realize you are engaging in destructive gossip about a fellow servant of Christ. Or you will forget to do a job you agreed to do. Or you will oppose the actions others suggest because you are secretly jealous of them. Then you will say to yourself, "Fine leader I am! I talk a good game, but that's all."

Yet you decide not to stew in your guilt. Turning to Christ, you acknowledge your sin. Christ then heals you, saying, "Go and sin no more." Or, failing to hear a clear word from Christ, you turn to a fellow Christian and talk through your situation. Again surprised by grace, you are awed by the power of God working in and through your friend. And you feel forgiven, restored, whole once more.

Churches embroiled in conflict sometimes call me for help. The bitterness I find, plus the hard feelings and blaming attitude, always stun me. I keep wondering to myself, "For starters, why don't they at least forgive each other? Have they never needed forgiveness? Or do they even know what forgiveness is?" *From time to time I have concluded that we Christians neglect the most remarkable power in the world, the power of forgiveness.* And as long as we live in our own little worlds, preoccupied with being right, neglecting to judge ourselves first in disputes, it will always be so. Something to think about, isn't it?

The Good News about Jesus

"Then Philip began to speak, and starting with this scripture, he proclaimed to him the good news about Jesus" (Acts 8:35). *Read Acts 8:26–40.*

Are you as astonished as I when you read this passage? What's *Philip* doing proclaiming the good news about Jesus to an Ethiopian eunuch? Wasn't he chosen to wait on tables? The apostles were supposed to proclaim the good news about Jesus. After all, they had called together the Christian community to choose seven men to distribute food. They said they wanted more time to pray and serve the word. Yet here is newly chosen Philip "serving the word" by proclaiming the good news about Jesus. What's going on, anyway?

Assuming a leadership position in the church never excuses us from proclaiming the good news about Jesus. Maybe the church primarily chose us to govern or usher or to keep records. No matter. God still wants us to be ready to proclaim the good news about Jesus' forgiveness and new life.

"All right," you say, "but witnessing is just not my thing." Granted, God may not have given you a particular *gift* for witnessing, but you still have a witnessing *role*. Don't we always need to be ready for God to call us to witness to someone as God called Philip? Shouldn't we be prepared to give a reason for the hope we found in Jesus? *Chosen primarily to wait on tables, Philip is best known because he proclaimed the good news about Jesus.*

Yes, we may feel totally inadequate and reluctant to proclaim the good news. Waiting on tables—serving—may be all the witnessing we think we should do. But don't be too sure! God may surprise you as God surprised Philip and tell you to proclaim the good news also. Serving *and* witnessing—both. No, you don't have to buttonhole people on street corners. Nor do you have to compulsively turn every airplane conversation into a discussion about your fellow passenger's eternal destiny. But quietly and unobtrusively you can share the reality of your faith in Christ as situations arise.

You never know what will happen when you start witnessing. After Philip baptized the eunuch and left, "*he proclaimed the good news to all the towns until he came to Caesarea*" (Acts 8:40b, italics mine). Once this waiter started telling others about Jesus he couldn't stop! May it be so for us, too.

Overcoming Evil with Good

"Do not be overcome by evil, but overcome evil with good" (Rom. 12:21). *Read Romans 12:14–21.*

A board member took me into his confidence. He said he wanted to make a statement to the board that would clarify and resolve some of the conflict we had been having in the church. "Trust me," he said. And so I did. When he later spoke at the meeting, he lambasted not only me but several other board members as well. Months later we were still reeling from the conflict that erupted. I was infuriated. I wanted to lash out at him and punish him. Then I remembered this verse: "Do not be overcome by evil, but overcome evil with good" (Rom. 12:21). The incident put my faith to the test, for I felt I had been betrayed.

Was Paul talking about enemies of the Christian faith *outside* the church or *inside*? Initially he probably meant enemies outside the church, but much that he wrote in this passage applies also to life within the church. "Live in harmony with another," he said. And, "live peaceably with all." Clearly, Paul included our relationships with persons inside the church, too.

And that's where our problem begins. We have enough trouble living in harmony with fellow church members without worrying about enemies outside the church. Don't board members sometimes undermine our leadership? Don't staff members talk behind our backs? Don't committee members fail to support the plans we make together? And when they do, we wish we had never heard of Paul. Or Jesus. We want to repay evil for evil. We are tempted to succumb to the same power that has gripped our enemies: *evil!* But if we do, we perpetuate, even escalate, a vicious circle of hate.

A true test of your leadership comes here. Do you allow evil to overcome you, or do you strive to overcome evil with good?

Let God help you overcome evil with good. How? Not by retaliating in kind. Not by repressing your anger and being nice.

No, confront the situation honestly. Urge people to disagree in love. Encourage them to play by the rules. And maybe you will overcome evil with good. If not, you will at least demonstrate that vengeance belongs to *God*, not to *you*.

In Whom There is No Deceit

"When Jesus saw Nathanael coming toward him, he said of him, 'Here is truly an Israelite in whom there is no deceit!'" (John 1:47). *Read John 1:43–47.*

His face is engraved on my memory. He promised me one thing but did another. Or did he just forget? Either way, I felt devalued, even violated. Such are always the results of *deceit*.

Have you ever found it so? It may happen in any church setting with almost any leader: He or she promises one thing but does another. And you soon learn not to trust such a person. What you see and hear is not what you get. Isn't it hard to work with leaders like that? Your heart is no longer in what you are doing. Your morale suffers. You only go through the motions of your work.

No wonder I pounced on this text with such gusto! About Nathanael, our Lord said, "Here is truly an Israelite *in whom there is no deceit!*" (Italics mine.) Jesus saw Nathanael under the fig tree before Philip called him to come and see Jesus. And Jesus concluded that Nathanael was without deceit. In other words, he saw someone who was sincere, genuine, honest, candid, and forthright. However we pile up these synonyms, they point to that rare person in whom there is no deceit.

The longer I work with church leaders, the more I'm convinced we need more Nathanaels around. To guide the work of the church, we need persons who relate to one another honestly and openly—with no deceit. Deceit is a poison pill that destroys human relationships. It can quickly undermine a staff, demoralize a board, or thwart a committee.

So as you lead, let your yes be yes and your no be no. Don't promise one thing and do another. Don't smile pleasantly to cover up a cauldron of hostility. Don't praise others effusively when you don't mean it. Be genuine. And, yes, you can do all of the above without being brutally frank.

But wait a minute! Can any leader stand up to such scrutiny?

Is there anyone with a perfect record? No. Thus we need to go and "see" Jesus, as did Nathanael. Jesus will always forgive us and help us live without deceit, as did Nathanael.

The Joy That Christ Gives

"I have said these things to you so that my joy may be in you, and that your joy may be complete" (John 15:11). *Read John 15:1–11.*

Long ago Jesus promised joy: "I have said these things to you so that my joy may be in you, and that your joy may be complete." And Jesus fulfills his promise—every time.

At youth conferences we used to sing: "I've got the joy of Jesus down in my heart." "Where?" we then asked. "Down in my heart!" we sang even louder. Yet, only now do I better understand why no other approach to life brings such deep, heartfelt joy.

The joy that Jesus gives is complete, indeed. Down through the ages people have found in him their reason for being. Jesus Christ satisfies the deepest needs of the human heart. And he gives us joy. His joy results from *abiding in him*. It's nurtured through *prayer*. And it's further nourished by *loving obedience to Jesus' commands*.

Which brings us to the point: Christian leaders need joy in their lives. Is it not a "fruit of the Spirit"? When we ground our lives in Jesus—abide in him—he gives us joy. And that characteristic is indispensable in doing the work of Christ. If we wear nothing but sad, stressed-out, tense faces, we will hardly inspire others to serve with us. But if we show enthusiasm and exude genuine joy, our manner will be contagious. Almost without knowing why, others will be eager to join us in serving Christ.

Note this: No one can push a button and produce joy. Do you remember the ultimate source of joy? We begin by abiding in Jesus, praying in his name, and obeying his commandments. Only then does Jesus promise us his *joy*. No shortcuts are possible. The joy springs from abiding in Jesus, the True Vine. It is the *fruit* of the vine, of course, not the vine itself.

Don't all of us need to learn this truth? Surely it would spare us a lifetime of trivial pursuits, as well as much of our anxious striving to squeeze the last ounce of pleasure out of life. And it would free us from succumbing to the pressure of countless ads that promise us joy only if we buy a certain product. Nothing else satisfies the restless heart like having the joy of Jesus down in our hearts!

The Peace of Christ

"Peace I leave with you; my peace I give to you. I do not give to you as the world gives" (John 14:27a). *Read John 14:25–31.*

As we approach the end of our lives, we often bequeath to others what we have learned and accumulated. Some simply gather together family and friends, share their wisdom, and exchange good-byes. Many write wills and establish trusts, deciding how they will allocate their possessions. Are not the final days a time to do what seems most important to us?

Jesus proved no exception. To his disciples, Jesus left this legacy: "Peace I leave with you; my peace I give to you." He had nothing else to leave. Money? He had none. Possessions? He had nothing except his clothing, and soon a crucifixion squad would gamble even that away. So Christ left his followers all that he had, his peace.

Yet no gift could have been as great as the peace of Christ. Not a huge trust fund. Not a beautiful estate. No, the peace of Christ is the bequest we most need.

The peace Christ gives is not a promise that we will have no trouble. Were we not "born to trouble just as sparks fly upward" (Job 5:7)? Certainly Christ himself was not spared trouble. Rather, he died with spit in his face and jeers ringing in his ears, yet saying, "Father, forgive them;

for they do not know what they are doing" (Luke 23:34). He had a peace that kept him steady even on a cruel cross.

The world promises peace through narcotics and idyllic lakeside cabins. Christ gives peace through his life, death, and resurrection. He frees us from sin and enables us to trust the same God who gave him peace at the end.

Is not the peace of Christ the gift leaders most need? How can we plan the work of the kingdom if we haven't received this peace "which surpasses all understanding"? But when we reflect this peace in our work, we will point others toward the reality for which we strive. *Suddenly leadership is more than a skill to be learned—it is based on a gift to be accepted.*

Sad to say, Jesus has some missing heirs. I am searching my heart to see if I am among them. How about you?

The Conviction of Things Not Seen

"By faith Abraham obeyed when he was called to set out for a place that he was to receive as an inheritance; and he set out, not knowing where he was going" (Heb. 11:8). *Read Hebrews 11:1–12.*

Trust and obey," we have sung, "for there's no other way." We trust in Jesus Christ as Lord and Savior. And we also trust that the God who has led us to faith will take care of us each day. But do we really believe that?

Every time I search for God's will and make a decision, I get scared. I wonder if I can believe God's promises. Oh, I can look back over my life and see clearly that God has been with me every step of the way. God has delivered on every promise. How could I ever doubt again? But when a new situation arises, I wonder all over again. A painful admission, but nonetheless true.

My wife Gail coordinates a night shelter for homeless women here in Atlanta. She ensures that volunteers are enlisted to spend the night and bring an evening meal for the women. But Gail has often seen her well-laid plans begin to fall apart. Volunteers move away or have emergencies or mixups. Then suddenly someone calls and offers to spend the night or provide a meal. So Gail concluded long ago that God will provide for that shelter!

Still, working in Christ's church is a constant test of faith. Will we be able to find someone to keep the nursery next Sunday? Will we receive a large enough offering to pay our bills? Will God be with us if we take a brave stand for the gospel? Will our new service project work out? Often we tremble while we wait to see what happens.

Such uncertainty scares us to death, because we want to know the future in advance. Frightened, we are afraid to launch out; we fear we will fail. But faith doesn't work that way. Rather, it launches us on a journey without our knowing how the plot will turn out. And God often calls us to move out of our comfort zones. We have no guarantees except that a promise-keeping God will be with us!

Christian leaders are persons of *faith*. Like Abraham long ago, they launch out in faith, not knowing where they are going. *But they do trust God.* They know that the One who has never let them down will be with them in the future. And because they trust God, they obey.

So must we!

Hope That Does Not Disappoint

"...but we also boast in our sufferings, knowing that suffering produces endurance, and endurance produces character, and character produces hope, and hope does not disappoint us..." (Rom. 5:3–5a). *Read Romans 5:1–5.*

For what do you hope? A college education? Marriage? Children? Grandchildren? A secure job? Good health care? Adequate retirement funds? You hope that what you desire has at least a chance of coming true or it wouldn't be hope.

Yet many people in our society have no hope. Trapped in a cycle of poverty or broken marriages or drug addiction, they say, "I have no hope." When people are hopeless, they gradually slip into despair. They can begin to march in the streets or resign themselves to a constant downward spiral.

Life itself has never seemed hopeless to me. Not that everything I hoped for came true! I think it's because of my "hope of sharing the glory of God," as Paul put it. (See Rom. 5:2.) Even when family and friends have died, I have not grieved "as others do who have no hope" (1 Thess. 4:13b). I know that beyond this life there is the "glory of God."

Throughout history, numerous Christian groups have thought that in death they could reach God, and so they took their own lives as a path to "the Father's kingdom." But Christians don't believe that God asks us to snuff out life to receive life. Rather, we accept the abundant life God gives us now, live it fully, and await the final glory of God when we die. We fall short of that glory now because of our sin, but someday we shall become the persons God intends us to be.

"How does hope relate to leadership?" you ask. Vitally. When we lead a church, much that we hope for does not work out. Or if it does, it happens only after intense struggle and conflict. But good leaders keep on keeping on because they hope to receive the glory of God. The love that the Holy Spirit has previously poured into their hearts is the basis for such strong hope in the future.

So when church work discourages you, take heart. You can face momentary setbacks, because you hope eventually to share the glory of God. And that hope will never disappoint us.

Diligent or Lackadaisical?

"We have gifts that differ according to the grace given to us: prophecy, in proportion to faith; ministry, in ministering...the leader, in diligence" (Rom. 12:6–8). *Read Romans 12:3–8.*

It's well known that God gives Christians special gifts to build up the church, the body of Christ. A teacher uses her gifts in teaching fifth graders in Sunday school. The compassionate in the church build a house for Habitat for Humanity with cheerfulness. And the leader, Paul says, uses the gift of leadership or administration "in diligence."

Note that Paul connects leadership with diligence, earnestness, zeal. And no wonder. Leadership and diligence go hand in hand. How can anyone lead without being *diligent?* One dictionary defines diligence as "persistent, attentive, and energetic application to a task."[5]

Leaders who are diligent make wonderful colleagues: You know they will do the research needed to make a decision. They will tackle what they agreed to do. They will be on time. They will try again if they fail to accomplish a task the first time. In short, they exhibit "persistent, attentive, and energetic application to a task."

Yet many persons in church leadership positions fail to be diligent. Instead of being persistent, attentive, and energetic as they address a church task, they become lackadaisical. As lackadaisical leaders—a contradiction in terms—they lack spirit and interest when they do church work. Need some examples?

At a board meeting, when several members request the worship committee to explore the possibility of going to two Sunday services, Henry says, "We haven't got time to deal with that issue. Why don't we leave well enough alone?" Henry simply doesn't want to do it.

Or at a staff meeting Pete reports that he was unable to complete his hospital calls because "something came up." But with Pete something always comes up.

Or Melanie, who habitually runs ten to fifteen minutes late for work, breathlessly says once again, "The traffic was really bad today!" And Melanie doesn't have the added responsibility of getting young children off to school as do other staff members.

No, no. Church leaders are *diligent*, not *lackadaisical*. How do you come out when the searchlight illumines your work?

Mature, Yet Immature

"Beloved, I do not consider that I have made it my own;
but this one thing I do:…I press on toward the
goal…Let those of us then who are mature be of the
same mind…" (Phil. 3:13–15).

W hen we think of mature people, do we not think of
people who are highly developed? They are together
persons who are wise, who don't jump to conclusions, and
who consider matters carefully before making decisions. Yet
here in Philippians we discover a paradox: *Christian leaders
who are most mature are at the same time most aware of their
immaturity!*

Consider Paul as exhibit A. The world has never seen a
more mature Christian than Paul. But in this text he
stresses that he has not achieved maturity, that he is a work
in progress. Twice he says things like "I do not consider
that I have made it my own…" Was he not saying that he
was incomplete, immature, imperfect? But how? Paul had
just said he wanted to know Christ and the power of his
resurrection. He also wanted to share in the sufferings of
Christ and to attain the resurrection from the dead. Thus
by admitting his immaturity, Paul was stating that he had
fallen short of experiencing Christ as much as he would
like. And that's a healthy and mature position for any
Christian leader to take.

Too often we expect our church leaders to be perfect
Christians. Unfortunately, some of them begin to think

they can be! I once met a man who tearfully said he was no longer perfect. He was crying because for five years, three months, and two days he had lived without sinning! Yet Paul himself forthrightly admitted his immaturity.

So do mature Christian leaders today. Not long after I graduated from seminary, I met one of my favorite professors at a church meeting. In an informal conversation afterward, he told some of us about his ongoing struggle with himself. I was surprised, for he was one of the most mature Christians I knew. But I shouldn't have been surprised, because his honesty demonstrated the very essence of Christian maturity. He was admitting, as did Paul, his immaturity.

Yet note this: Paul said he was pressing on toward the goal, straining like a runner for the finish line. Far from being discouraged or paralyzed by his immaturity, he used it as an incentive to press on "for the prize of the heavenly call of God in Christ Jesus" (Phil. 3:14). As for me, I want to follow and work with leaders who are mature, yet who know that they are immature. How about you?

A Leader is... Trustworthy

"Timothy, guard what has been entrusted to you"
(1 Tim. 6:20). *Read 1 Timothy 6:17–21.*

When I consider leadership qualities, I immediately think about trust. How important it is to be able to trust our church leaders. No one can lead us effectively without our confidence. And once our trust has been shattered, it's hard to establish it again.

In today's brief passage Timothy is enjoined to guard what has been entrusted to him—the Christian faith. He is instructed to faithfully pass on the gospel he learned from his grandmother Lois and his mother Eunice. (See also 2 Tim. 1:5.) *That* faith now lived in Timothy, and he needed to share it with others. And he could do so only by continuing to live it and proclaim it *faith*fully.

Thus it is with us who lead the church now. We sometimes forget that the bottom line of all that we do is to guard what has been entrusted to us—the Christian faith. But how quickly that purpose gets lost in our church meetings and activities! Frustrated and angry with one another, we sometimes give up. Or by our actions we may even betray the very faith we are commissioned to transmit. When we do, we are hardly guarding what has been entrusted to us.

How crucial it is for us church leaders, then, to live the faith that we seek to transmit. Only in that way can we build a relationship of trust with our members. Out of that trust we can develop a strong program of Christian nurture, build vital staff relationships, and govern the church wisely. Without it we will certainly flounder.

Her question stunned me. On the last day of a doctor of ministry course I was teaching, Frances suddenly asked, "Are you as you seem to be?" After taking a deep breath, I realized she was asking, "Can we trust you?" I discovered that a previous instructor told them to write a paper in a certain way but graded them by different criteria. Thus the students' confidence was shaken; they sought assurance that I was trustworthy. I hope that my subsequent actions reassured them.

"A Scout is trustworthy..." Many of us learned to repeat that years ago at scout meetings. As well, a Christian leader is trustworthy. We guard the faith that has been entrusted to us by living and proclaiming it faithfully. I tremble at this responsibility. But I am steadied when once again I place my *trust* in our *trustworthy* God who helps us guard the *trust* of the gospel.

Faith, Hope, Love: And the Winner Is...

"And now faith, hope, and love abide, these three; and the greatest of these is love" (1 Cor. 13:13). *Read 1 Corinthians 13:8–14a.*

Ah, Paul's hymn to love: We quote it, read it in marriage ceremonies, and talk about its beauty. There in the heart of the New Testament is one of the most incredible passages in all literature. It's so beautiful, in fact, that we get caught up in its soaring phrases and overlook the actual meaning of the verses.

When I was a boy, I used to quote 1 Corinthians 13 like everyone else. Now I see it quite differently. I read it and want to weep. For whenever I ponder the meaning of these verses I notice how much I fail to live by their reality.

For an experiment, read verses 4–7 again and substitute your name for the word love every time it appears. For example, I would say, "Bob is patient; Bob is kind; Bob is not envious or boastful or arrogant or rude." When I substitute my name, suddenly everything changes! I remember *my* impatience with a staff member. I recall an episode when *I* was too busy to be kind. I think about *my* envy of colleagues. And so on until I say, "Stop! I've had enough. I can't live by these verses."

Look at your church relationships now in the same light. As you substitute your name for love, ask yourself if you are patient with your board or staff or committee. Have you been kind? Have you been envious or arrogant or rude? Perhaps Paul's hymn of love is now as disturbing to you as it is to me! You realize how hard it is to love one another consistently. Family and friends? Maybe. Fellow church workers? Sometimes. People you don't know, including enemies and strangers? Now this is rapidly becoming a difficult passage, isn't it? We don't come out too well. You and I know we need the forgiveness of Christ for our failure to love as we ought.

"What the world needs now is love, sweet love," we sang a few years ago. The older we get, the more we know that the world really does need more love.

Faith, the trust in Jesus Christ that saves us, is great. So is hope, the hope we have for the glory of God. Yet the greatest of these is love. So follow Paul's advice and "pursue love." Love will never end.

PART 3

Christian Leadership Skills

God's Servants, Working Together

"For we are God's servants, working together" (1 Cor. 3:9a). *Read 1 Corinthians 3:1–9.*

What a difference it would make in the church if we could see ourselves as "God's servants, working together." Yet both service and collaboration are difficult for us.

Surely it's hard to see ourselves as servants when we want to be number one. Daily the cry goes up across our land, "We're number one!" You see it on television and in the movies; you read it in the newspaper; you hear it on your radio. Everybody wants to be number one. But here, Paul comes along and says that he and Apollos are God's *servants*. "I planted," continues Paul, "Apollos watered, but God gave the growth" (1 Cor. 3:6). "So neither the one who plants nor the one who waters is anything, but only God who gives the growth" (1 Cor. 3:7). When will we learn to plant and water God's field and let God grow it? *We* are servants.

But we are more than servants; we are servants *working together.* Don't we need to collaborate? Of course, you may be able to do some things even better than a group can. Yet, most of the time, "All of us are smarter than any one of us." We make better decisions because we study all sides of an issue, reflect different viewpoints, and affirm everyone involved. "A camel is a racehorse designed by a committee," we joke. Though sometimes true, that is a lighthearted comment with little substance.

Yes, collaborating takes time and effort. It's not easy to coordinate the talents and gifts of all involved. But when we do justice to the process, seek input from everyone, evaluate proposed solutions carefully, choose the best solution, and prepare to put into action what we've decided, collaboration can be exhilarating.

Dean Smith, famed basketball coach at the University of North Carolina, was at his self-effacing best when he became the winningest coach in NCAA history. Smith was obviously happier for all of his teams than he was for himself. In sports, as in life, he was living proof that players win as a team, not as individual stars. Smith proved, incidentally, that one can be number one and still be a *servant of the team.*

In a church setting, working together—and as *God's* servants—is the path to follow.

Sober Judgment

"For by the grace given to me I say to everyone among you not to think of yourself more highly than you ought to think, but to think with sober judgment..."(Rom. 12:3). *Read Romans 12:1–3.*

Here are Bill Marriott's keys to better relationships:

The six most important words: *I admit that I was wrong.*

The five most important: *You did a great job.*

The four most important: *What do you think?*

The three most important: *Could you, please?*

The two most important: *Thank you.*

The most important: *We.*

The least important: *I.*[6]

What remarkable advice! Marriott succinctly stresses several keys to better relationships: thinking properly about yourself, as well as respecting and affirming others.

How important it is to think about ourselves with sober judgment, yet we often fall into pride and think more highly of ourselves than we ought to think. Can we ever admit that we were wrong? On the other hand, we can also fall off the proverbial horse on the other side and slip into sloth, thinking less of ourselves than we should. So many of us in the church don't have good opinions of ourselves despite hearing all our lives that we were created in God's own image.

But neither falling into pride nor slipping into sloth is the *proper* way to estimate ourselves. In other words, we all have a contribution to make so we must make it. After all, Christ has given each of us gifts to use for building up the church, his body.

Yet as we contribute, remember that we do belong to a body. Others also have gifts to offer. It's therefore essential for us to respect others, saying please and thank you as Bill Marriott suggested and as our mothers taught us! And isn't it also necessary to work with others, asking their opinions —what do you think?—and affirming their contributions —you did a great job.

Reflect then on your work relationships. Are you thinking more highly of yourself than you ought to think? And are you respecting and affirming others enough?

Good questions, these. Ponder them.

Learning to Delegate

"Moses' father-in-law said to him, 'What you are doing is not good. You will surely wear yourself out, both you and these people with you. For the task is too heavy for you; you cannot do it alone'" (Exod. 18:17–18). Read Exodus 18:13–27.

R ecently a businessman said about one of his employees: "The trouble with Terry is that he tries to do everything himself. He has never learned to delegate."

More than one minister has resigned in frustration and burnout, admitting, "I've never learned to delegate."

How many committee members lose interest in the work of their committee, exclaiming, "Our chair never calls a meeting and always insists on doing everything"?

Moses particularly had this problem. People streamed in to see him everyday to seek God's will in disputes that arose. And Moses "made known to them the statutes and instructions of God" (Exod. 18:16). There was only one difficulty: He was wearing himself out. Jethro, Moses' father-in-law, wisely told him to delegate, for the task was too heavy for him to do alone. Isn't it amazing that Moses listened to his *father-in-law*, chose able, trustworthy, and honest men to help him, trained them, and delegated to them part of his responsibilities? And the plan worked!

But notice that Moses chose able, trustworthy, and honest people. He also trained them to make wise decisions for God. He further told them to bring important cases to him. In other words, Moses himself did not delegate and then retire to sit on the sidelines. Rather, he became a teacher and continued to decide important cases.

Delegation still works. Are you in a leadership position? If so, reflect on these questions: Do you need to learn to delegate? Are you wearing yourself out? Why and how? Will you choose mature people—able, trustworthy, honest —to help you? Will you train them? And will you continue to support them in their work and be actively involved in making decisions?

Of one thing I'm sure: Many modern church leaders desperately need to learn from Jethro and Moses. Church work will surely wear you out if you try to do it alone.

Listen to Me!

"The whole assembly kept silence, and listened to Barnabas and Paul as they told of all the signs and wonders that God had done through them among the Gentiles" (Acts 15:12). *Read Acts 15:6–22.*

That early council meeting in Jerusalem has always impressed me. Convened to resolve burning issues in the infant Christian church, the council revealed many qualities that we should emulate. Among them was this: "The whole assembly kept silence, and listened to Barnabas and Paul..." Of all the dynamics that came into play at the meeting, keeping silence and listening were in the "Top Ten."

Even keeping silence in itself is a monumental task for us!

When others are speaking, we sometimes interrupt them in the middle of a sentence. And almost as rude is our tendency to plan what we want to say before they finish.

But merely keeping silence is only the beginning of treating others fairly. You can do that without ever really *listening* to a thing they say. When you listen to others, you nod and say, "I see," to let them know you are with them. You also understand both the *content* of what they say and the *feeling* behind the content. "You are angry when reports are always late." Late reports constitute the content, anger the feeling. And when the person speaking says, "Yes, that's exactly what I mean," then you have understood. Certainly we owe one another that much if we in turn wish to speak and be understood.

Did that famous Jerusalem council listen as I have described it? Perhaps not. After all, they did not copy down what they heard, or use insight from the study of psychology, or attend parent effectiveness training, or read books about resolving church conflict. *Yet they were knit together in bonds of Christian fellowship.* They loved both the Lord and one another. And that was enough to encourage them to listen respectfully. Their careful listening helped them solve two thorny issues: how Gentiles could convert to the Christian faith and also how they could have table fellowship with Jews.

"Listen to me," is a universal cry. We want to be heard, we need to be heard. When we know that others have really listened to us, then we will work with them even though our ideas may not prevail.

So, how can we ever lead unless we learn to listen? Do you hear what I'm saying?

Bearing Burdens

"Bear one another's burdens, and in this way you will fulfill the law of Christ" (Gal. 6:2). *Read Galatians 6:1–5.*

Does the title put you off? After all, burdens weigh us down. But that's just the point. Sooner or later all of us become weighed down by the burdens of life. We stagger beneath the load of job stress, family discord, financial problems, physical or mental illness, and community conflict. Their weight seems more than we can bear. At other times we carry the load, but need someone to place a hand beneath it and hold it up for awhile. Both occur often in the church.

At a staff meeting, when personal concerns are shared, Beth mentions that her mother will enter the hospital for tests on a suspicious lump. At a board meeting Hal says he is having trouble recruiting enough people to help with the church picnic. Before her committee meets, Martha asks her pastor for help in learning how to chair the meeting.

Some of the burdens we face are deeply troubling, while others are mere "gnat bites." Yet even gnats make you feel bad when they attack in swarms! Both the deeply troubling burdens and gnat bites cause us to welcome the help of others. "Give us a hand," we say. And our fellow church workers pitch in and help, believing the old adage,

"Many hands make light work." Others bear our burdens and so fulfill the law of Christ—loving one another.

Right here, however, is where many of us fail. Burdened ourselves, don't we tend to say, "I've got enough problems of my own. Someone else will have to help"? That argument sounds quite plausible until *we* get in trouble. Then we cast about, looking for help anywhere we can find it!

Of course, there's a limit to the amount of help we can and should give for others' sake and ours. Eventually, as the text reminds us: "All must carry their own loads" (Gal. 6:5). Thus it's important for us not to overload our fellow workers. It will cripple our work relationships if we are too dependent on them.

In the meantime, though, we can help others in the church by being sensitive to their distress signals, understanding and clarifying their needs, readily sharing useful information, identifying resources, and following up with them later to express interest in how things are going. Have you borne any such burdens lately?

The Encourager

"There was a Levite, a native of Cyprus, Joseph, to whom the apostles gave the name Barnabas (which means 'son of encouragement')" (Acts 4:36). *Read Acts 4:32–37.*

B ible characters fascinate us. All of us have our favorites, depending on who we are and how we see life. Barnabas is one of my favorites.

A native of Cyprus, Barnabas was originally named Joseph. But the apostles gave him a new name, which means "son of encouragement." And encourage, he did.

Whenever a person or a cause needed a boost, Barnabas was there to give it. Were there needy persons among them? All right, Barnabas sold a field and gave the money to the apostles to meet their need. Did young John Mark need encouragement after he deserted Paul and Barnabas on one of their journeys? Again, Barnabas stood behind him and wanted to give him another chance. So much so that he parted company with Paul and sailed away to Cyprus *with Mark.* The encourager at work once more!

Don't we need more Barnabases around our churches? We have more than enough negative, demanding, scolding, and complaining people among us. We need men and women who stand with us, saying, "You can do it, I know you can." Our times require people who step forward at precisely the right moment and say the right thing or put their money on the line.

Sooner or later we all need the support of an encourager. My phone rang the morning after a highly conflicted board meeting that left me bruised and discouraged. Leon said, "I just wanted you to know that I was thinking about you this morning. I know the meeting was rough on you." My pain didn't vanish instantly, but the burden lifted, nonetheless. *I knew that someone cared about me and believed in me.* And that was the encouragement I needed to get through the day.

All wise leaders encourage those with whom they work. Of course, they don't condone incompetence or sloppy work. But they are willing to stand with others and help them try again. And what a difference that can make. Remember John Mark? The one-time deserter became a gospel writer. That was surely the biblical comeback of the year!

Expecting Excellence

"According to the grace of God given to me, like a skilled master builder I laid a foundation, and someone else is building on it" (1 Cor. 3:10). *Read 1 Corinthians 3:10–15.*

When we recruit Sue for a church job, aren't we tempted to say, "It won't take much time"? And when Bill doesn't do his job well, don't we say to ourselves, "What can you expect, he is only a volunteer"?

It stretches my imagination to realize what low expectations we place on church work. We seem to expect mediocrity, so what do we get? Mediocrity! Put that down as a law of the church—and of life, for that matter.

At first glance we excuse poor work out of our compassion. After all, church members are often busy. They are involved in their home life, their jobs, and their community activities. "Handle with care," we say, trying to be sensitive to their needs.

Now I'll be the first to tell you that church life can absolutely overwhelm you. *But only if you let it.* As a minister I quickly found out there's always more to do than one can possibly do. Thus every minister, every church leader, and every member has to take time for self and family and say no when necessary.

That said, don't go overboard to protect people. *Christ* called us to serve. We are thus more than volunteers, for we have become captive to him. In his service is our real freedom. *And life in his service requires us to give our very best in all that we do for him.*

Paul likened his work as a missionary preacher to a skilled master builder. Note the word "skilled." Not *mediocre*, but *skilled.* The Christ who called Paul into his service expected him to be the best he could be.

Likewise, the Christ who calls us expects us to be skilled in what we do. So learn how to lead. Learn how to work together. And learn how to do your job better. Are we not engaged in the most important work in the world? Then we dare not give it less than our best.

"Each builder must choose with care how to build on" other foundations, Paul said. (1 Cor. 3:10b). Choose with care indeed how you build!

Where There is No Vision

"Where there is no vision, the people perish"
(Prov. 29:18, KJV). *Read Proverbs 29:11–18, KJV.*

What's true in business is also true in the church: "Where there is no vision, the people perish." This older translation of Proverbs 29:18 in the King James Version has become so embedded in popular culture that we revisit it today.

A vision is more than a wish, even more than a dream. For a wish can be cast aside, and a dream can merely cling to the emotions and paralyze a congregation. Not so a vision. *A vision is a clear picture of what God wants a church to do.* Moreover, it's powerful enough to mobilize ample resources to make the vision come true.

A true vision *originates* when either a leader or a member discerns God's will. It *advances* when church leaders communicate the vision to the congregation. It *produces* when leaders and members turn it into reality.

Note well that vision never arises from leaders alone. Some leaders are simply not very visionary! But it doesn't matter as long as they help the congregation to be visionary. Does not every congregation contain devout souls who are seeking God's will for their church? So allow their vision to surface. And if the Spirit helps you see its wisdom, share it with others.

Also observe that without the support of the congregation, visions can turn into white elephants. While visionary leaders are often right, they can also be quite wrong. Mammoth building projects, without significant congregational endorsement, can leave a church financially strapped for years. In other words, the people must share the vision of the one who sees it. It must become their vision, too.

So what vision does God have for your church? What does God want your church to become? Are you, as leaders, regularly looking at your congregational life in light of scripture? Are you helping members also to seek God's will for your life together?

But discerning God's dream for your church does not end the process. The vision must become a reality. And it will not become a reality until the people freely and enthusiastically embrace the power of that corporate dream.

From Vision to Mission

> "During the night Paul had a vision: there stood a man of Macedonia pleading with him and saying, 'Come over to Macedonia and help us'" (Acts 16:9). *Read Acts 16:6–10.*

It's one thing to see a vision of God's will, yet quite another to act on it. The vision must be translated into reality—from vision to mission. So it was for Paul.

While ministering in Troas with missionary companions Silas and Timothy, Paul had a vision. There stood a man pleading with him, saying, "Come over to Macedonia and help us." How easy it would have been for Paul to ignore his vision. "I was only dreaming," we might have said. But not Paul. With his companions he acted on the vision and *entered Europe for the first time,* going into Macedonia. They acted on Paul's vision, because they were convinced that *God* had called them to proclaim the good news. (See Acts 16:10.)

Do you see the progression from vision to mission? God called Paul in a vision—they were convinced of that. They then took action and set sail for Macedonia.

I graduated from Hampden-Sydney College, a small Presbyterian school in central Virginia. As I write, the president of Hampden-Sydney is a deeply committed Presbyterian elder named Samuel V. Wilson. A retired general, President Wilson possesses extraordinary vision. His long-range "vision" for the school is to increase the endowment from the current $65 million to $100 million by the year 2000. "When I dropped that figure in a committee meeting several years ago, it was met with gasps," Wilson says. "But I felt we must have it simply to prevent our falling behind. Now, $100 million is becoming an increasingly realistic figure."[7] Many people have now enthusiastically adopted Wilson's vision and are making it come true.

But so often in our churches we gasp at the dreams of others, then dismiss them. "Dreamers," we say derisively. Or our characteristic knee-jerk reaction when someone proposes anything is to ask, "How much will it cost?" Shouldn't we *first* judge the desirability and validity of a vision and *then* inquire about its cost? *Remember: God may be the source of the vision.* And God may want you to help make it come true.

Decisions, Decisions!

"Therefore I have reached the decision that we should not trouble those Gentiles who are turning to God…" (Acts 15:19a).

D ecisions, decisions," we sometimes sigh. Doesn't it seem that we are always in a decision-making mode? Which movie to see? What to do about a family discipline problem? How to cope with job demands?

It's no different in the church. What decisions do you face right now? What to do about that staff situation? How best to deal with declining attendance? Which plans to adopt? The list is endless.

As leaders, you play a prominent role in decision making. You decide *how you will make decisions*—by vote, consensus, or unanimous consent. You decide *who will make decisions*—an individual, a small group, the leaders only, or the leaders with input by other participants. You decide *what data you need to collect*. You decide *how you will carry out the decision*. Yes, decisions, decisions!

Need some suggestions? Find out first how you make decisions right now. Track the actual process you follow in your board, staff, group, and congregation. Are people truly heard? Are feelings expressed? Is the decision later monitored to see how it's being implemented?

Next, let the nature of the task determine the process. Sensitive personnel matters, technical problems, and property issues can often be initially delegated to a few. A major building program, however, invites widespread participation at various levels. Of course, your form of church government often regulates the entire process.

Finally, the size of the group affects decision making. You use voting rather than consensus in groups of 500, for example. Conversely, you should allow a small group to discuss in-depth personnel issues.

Our text says that *James*, Jesus' brother and head of the church in Jerusalem, reached the decision concerning the Gentiles. Perhaps he summed up what everyone was saying and proposed a compromise that was accepted. But he was not alone. The apostles and elders had met together to debate the issues. Moreover, the whole church decided unanimously how they should implement the decision not to saddle the Gentiles with all the details of the Mosaic law.

So make your decisions carefully. Few things create more unnecessary conflict and resentment than sloppy procedures![8]

Gathering Input to Discern God's Will

"For it has seemed good to the Holy Spirit and to us to impose on you no further burden than these essentials…" (Acts 15:28). *Read Acts 15:22–29.*

As we have noted, *careful listening* helped the Jerusalem council resolve two thorny issues: how Gentiles could convert to the Christian faith and also how they could have table fellowship with them. Now we look again at the dynamics behind these important decisions.

To resolve such thorny issues the council members gathered input from the Holy Spirit as well as one another. They heard Peter tell how the Gentiles had received the Holy Spirit. And they believed that the Spirit was at work among them, guiding them to discern the divine will.

But in our "solemn assemblies" don't we sometimes tack on the necessity of seeking guidance from the Holy Spirit? Don't we really think we will hammer out the issues *by our own might and power?*

Perhaps I am merely projecting my own tendencies upon the group process. For I know how often I grind out my work in true do-it-yourself fashion, as though everything depends upon me. But when I begin in prayer, my work and my day somehow go better. In my own experience I have discovered the mysterious guidance of the Spirit who intercedes for us when we hardly know what and how to pray. And what holds true for us as individuals certainly holds true for church groups also. So seek input from the Holy Spirit in your meetings.

Then seek input from one another. As you listen to one another, look for merit in the ideas others express. Even if you disagree with them, make sure that each person is clearly heard and understood.

Moreover, learn how to "piggyback" on the ideas of others. You can say, "Valerie, your idea has triggered another thought in me. Maybe we could have the Bible study you suggest but incorporate it into our Sunday school program." If the group finally adopts the Sunday school Bible study, Valerie will know that she has contributed to the plan. She will feel valued by her colleagues. But it will have taken both you and Valerie to come up with the final result, *and the Holy Spirit working in and through all of you as you meet.*

After all of your meetings, may you be able to say, "It has seemed good to the Holy Spirit and to us…"

Reconciliation: Ministry and Gift

"All this is from God, who reconciled us to himself
through Christ, and has given us the ministry of
reconciliation" (2 Cor. 5:18).

For many years I have taught courses in conflict management. People are always interested in the subject,
because they all have conflicts. And they want help! Of the
principles we discuss, this one receives the biggest response:
"Theologically we can say that reconciliation, like grace, is
a gift…Thus, our 'work' in conflict management cannot be
the creating of reconciliation. That is God's work."[9]

This statement from Speed Leas rightly points out that
we cannot make reconciliation happen, no matter how
hard we try. If people in the church are reconciled to one
another, it has to be God's work, God's *gift*. But we do have
a *ministry* of reconciliation, as Paul put it. In our ministry
we can work to create an environment in which God may
grant us the gift of reconciliation.

One of my conflict management courses became
conflicted indeed. But I asked for it. I knew that unless I
allowed the growing conflict in the group to surface I
would not be teaching effectively. So I passed out an
inventory that permitted students to identify how well we
were working together. And they told me! They were
particularly upset with one member of the group for
talking too much. In turn the talkative member was deeply

offended by the exercise and angrily said so. At the next session, he refused to speak and even dozed off.

The rest of the class was almost as upset as I. I could see the whole course sinking like the *Titanic*.

What to do? One member tried to force reconciliation by inviting the offended member to work the issue with us, but he wasn't ready to do so. When we invited him to go to lunch, he said no. *All we could do was to be patient and open and to pray for reconciliation.* That was our ministry.

As we prayed for healing to come among us, we felt helpless at times. We saw exactly what Speed Leas meant: *We could not make reconciliation happen.* But God could and did. When we met several weeks later, the offended member asked for our forgiveness. And we asked for his as well. We experienced God's grace once again and became reconciled. It was indeed a powerful moment.

When you are estranged from one another, perform your *ministry* of reconciliation. Then pray mightily for God's *gift* to come among you!

Abused but Not Abusive

"When he was abused, he did not return abuse; when he suffered, he did not threaten; but he entrusted himself to the one who judges justly" (1 Peter 2:23).

In this century we have witnessed remarkable demonstrations of human courage. Mohandas K. Gandhi showed it in India by reacting to violence with nonviolence. Martin Luther King, Jr., later did the same thing when facing hostile mobs during the Civil Rights movement. Both reacted lovingly to what was done to them.

Of course, Jesus showed the way long ago. He *taught* the way of love, saying, "Love your enemies and pray for those who persecute you" (Matt. 5:44). And Jesus *lived* the way of love. When crucified, he even prayed for God to forgive his tormentors. "When he was abused," as Peter put it, "he did not return abuse."

Perhaps these examples seem a far cry from your church experience. You don't keep an enemies list, and you may never have faced what you would call persecution. But our enemies may be any threatening physical, social, and economic conditions we think will undo us. For example, church leaders complain that their congregations do not give enough to finance the church's programs. Or, they say that the neighborhood is changing so there's nothing they can do. Or, they blame the staff for not providing better direction. In addition to abusing others by blaming and complaining, they wring their hands in despair about conditions they think are beyond their control.

"It's not what happens to us, but our response to what happens to us that hurts us," writes Stephen Covey.[10] Viktor Frankl, a prisoner in the Nazi death camps, discovered in those human horror chambers that the Nazis could not take away his freedom to choose his response to what they did. Covey and Frankl point the way for modern leaders who want to be proactive instead of reactive, who choose to respond positively to negative circumstances.[11]

Church leaders would do well to learn these lessons. Lesson #1: You have the freedom to respond to what happens to you. Lesson #2: You can even respond in love to those who persecute you or speak ill of you. Through it all you will remember that when abused—attacked, criticized, or ignored—you will not return abuse. Instead, you will respond lovingly and creatively. Think about these things the next time you are tempted to blame unfavorable conditions for your situation and sit around doing nothing!

PART 4

Issues for
Christian
Leaders

No Conflict in the Church?

"For as long as there is jealousy and quarreling among you, are you not of the flesh, and behaving according to human inclinations?" (1 Cor. 3:3). Read 1 Corinthians 3:1–4.

I don't like to see any conflict in the church," an active church member said to me one day. "I have conflict everywhere else in my life but when I go to church, I don't want to see any conflict there."

No conflict in the church? Impossible, unless you turn all church members into *perfect* Christians! For the people who come to church are some of the same people you work with on the job, meet on the softball field, and live with at home. When they enter the sanctuary on Sunday, they do not suddenly become different people. They often include the very people who created havoc on the assembly line, yelled at the umpire on Wednesday night, and pouted at home. So how could we *not* have conflict in the church?

We will always have conflict in the church. It's normal and inevitable. Not pleasant, yes, but to be expected. You will see it break out in board meetings as you discuss the issues of the day. You will watch it erupt in staff meetings. And you will observe it popping up in committee work. Conflict happens in the church—count on it!

If conflict is inevitable, the real question is this: What will we do about it? We can face it openly and not run away. We can fight fairly without attacking one another. We can seek the mind of Christ. We can remember who we are and whom we serve. And when community breaks down, we can work toward reconciliation by forgiving one another and seeking constructive solutions.

"Jealousy and quarreling" surfaced in the Corinthian church, Paul noted. Factions became divisive, with one group wanting to follow Paul, another Apollos. Paul reminded them that all leaders serve *God* who makes growth possible. So it's our job to do our part and not worry about who gets the credit. Now that's easier to say than to do! For we long to receive the credit we think we deserve. Yet mature leaders can relax even when others get "high fives" for seeds the leaders themselves may have sown long ago.

Still, petty jealousy and quarreling constantly tear the fabric of church life. We leaders always need the forgiveness of the gospel we proclaim.

The Church: A Body, A System

"Now you are the body of Christ and individually members of it" (1 Cor. 12:27). *Read 1 Corinthians 12:14–31.*

A few years ago I began to study the church as a system. I was intrigued by the new lenses that the systems theory gave me for seeing the church. Yet my new lenses only gave me a fresh perspective on an old concept, the church as a body.

Said Paul to the Corinthians: "Now you are the body of Christ and individually members of it." He had just said that each one of them was a member of the body of Christ—a hand, or an eye, or a foot. And each member was indispensable for the life of the body. Further, if one suffered, all suffered. If one was honored, all rejoiced. (1 Cor. 12:26) Every person affected the whole body, and, conversely, the body affected every person. In other words, *they were interconnected in a system.* Yet modern systems theory helps us better understand this old idea of Paul.

Systems act like individual persons.[12] They are more than the sum of the individuals who make up the system. Thus a church group may make decisions for their group life that no person in that group would necessarily make as an individual.

Systems always resist change, *whether good or bad,* because they like to stay the same. No wonder it's hard to change things in the church!

Systems use people to keep everything in balance. If a key member of a church board leaves or dies, someone else will move into the vacuum and take up that person's cause.

Systems are affected by the family life of individuals.[13] Ever been puzzled when a husband and wife in your church unexpectedly attack the minister? Are they "triangling" the minister to stabilize their own shaky relationship?

Systems assign roles to their members. Some function as "parents" while others act as "children." Sound familiar? Suddenly the church system—more accurately, the body of Christ—takes on new meaning. Eyes, hands, feet—all are knit together in surprising and wondrous ways.

"Now you are the body of Christ and individually members of it."

Do It My Way!

"Love...does not insist on its own way..." (1 Cor. 13:4).
Read 1 Corinthians 13:4–7.

S ome people live out the slogan, "There's a right way, a wrong way, and *my* way." Living by that slogan has crippled the effectiveness of many church groups.

This widespread problem has been called *overcontrolling*. Need some examples? They aren't hard to find.

Overcontrolling affects church staffs as both clergy and support staff try rigidly to dominate everything they touch.

Overcontrolling affects church boards who use their power and authority to reject every new idea that surfaces.

Overcontrolling affects committee chairpersons who make sure that their wills prevail.

And we always resent overcontrolling, saying, "He sets the agenda and expects us to buy it automatically," or, "She has to do it her way," or, "I am told what I must do in every phase of my job, and how to do it."

Those who overcontrol assume that their way is *the* way. So they disregard what has been done in the past. They ignore what others think. "Do it *my* way," they shout.

In one survey overcontrolling was the key factor in 19 percent of church staff conflicts.[14] When I consult with churches, I often hear this complaint. Is there any hope of lessening tight control and opening up our processes? Of course. Ask these questions often in your church meetings:

How are we working together?

What are we trying to accomplish?

What is helping, and what is blocking us?

Discussing such questions won't eliminate overcontrolling, yet it may reduce it. The result of your work together will then be *your* way. Even more, hope and pray it will be *God's* way. Either way, "Love...does not insist on its own way."

Love Is Not Touchy

"[Love] is not touchy" (1 Cor. 13:5, Phillips). *Read 1 Corinthians 13:4–7.*

The NRSV translates this same verse: "It is not irritable..." (1 Cor. 13:5). But the Phillips translation immediately grabs me by nuancing irritability as being touchy.

Ever thought of touchiness as a sin? Probably not, but it can be. I don't know about you but I get touchy when I'm out of communion with God. I get touchy when I feel guilty. I get touchy when I'm tired and overloaded. I get touchy when you know more about me than I want you to know. I get touchy when I feel I haven't done a good job. And you?

Touchiness usually proves to be a downer for all relationships. Surely the church is no exception. How much human energy do we expend dealing with touchy people? They are so defensive, so quick to react that we constantly wonder how we can avoid setting them off. They wear their feelings on their sleeves. "Don't bring up that subject. That will only push her button," or, "Don't do that. It will throw him into a tirade." How often do we tiptoe around the touchy? It's like trying to walk on a carton of eggs without breaking one!

So what to do? For starters, always be sensitive to the feelings of others. Now that's both caring and wise. But also note that we can become *so* sensitive that we waste far too much energy and time protecting others—and ourselves—from their touchy responses.

Here's where I've come out: If I've been duly aware of the feelings of others, I have to take the risk of provoking their touchiness. They have to deal with it. After all, there's work to be done, and we can't forever tiptoe around their touchiness. We are responsible for facing difficult situations and considering the good of all the people of God. If we don't, we stifle our work and thus impede our mission in the kingdom of God. It's not right to allow the hypersensitivity of one or two people to shut down all hope of progress in a church. But I know how sticky it can get, especially when the touchy ones also donate a lot of money! I have struggled with this problem often.

Admittedly, my answer may not satisfy you. I invite you to write me your answer. But be careful—I'm touchy about how you critique *my* work!

Tending the Flock of God

> "...I exhort the elders among you to tend the flock of
> God that is in your charge, exercising the oversight, not
> under compulsion but willingly..." (1 Pet. 5:1b–2a).
> *Read 1 Peter 5:1–11.*

"Tend the flock of God," Peter said to elders scattered outside Palestine in the Dispersion.

Now some of you may not call yourselves elders. But whatever your title, you have church responsibilities for the flock of God. You exercise oversight within your sphere of activity. Thus you have a job to do, and you need to do it effectively. Certainly we can't condone outright neglect of people or a job. Is not competence important in the church?

But we often come up short on competence. In a church staff survey, 36 percent of *conflicted* staffs listed ineffectiveness as the number one problem.[15] Not only do some heads of staff complain about the competence of associates, but associates, complain about heads of staff as well.

Now broaden the application of competence to church boards and committees. How many of them are tending the flock of God diligently and effectively? Do they pray for the flock each day? Do they call or visit when grief crushes them? Do they support and guide them in their work in the world? Do they make decisions that reflect their input? Many church workers stumble over these questions.

Also involved in competence is our *attitude* toward church work. "Exercise the oversight, not under compulsion but willingly," Peter also says. Does not attitude influence effectiveness? For if our job attitude is bad and we don't really want to do it, then we aren't likely to perform well. Sometimes we may literally gnash our teeth when we accept a task in the church. We may even agree to do it only because the nominating committee couldn't find anyone else! How then can we ever expect to do a very good job when we resent it so much?

So as we look at our church work, let's be honest about both our competence and our attitude. Tending the flock of God is crucial in the kingdom. We can hardly proceed with our mission in the world if our own members are suffering from neglect. Learn then from Jesus, the Chief Shepherd, who laid his life down for the flock of God.

God's Faithfulness and Ours

"I will sing of your steadfast love, O LORD, forever; with my mouth I will proclaim your faithfulness to all generations" (Ps. 89:1). *Read Psalm 89:1–4.*

Some church leaders simply can't be counted on! There are ministers who don't do what they say they will do. They don't go to meetings. Or if they go, they are always late. They don't tell their office staff where they are going, nor do they promptly answer their mail and phone calls.

But also reflect on the conduct of members of boards, committees, and church staffs. When the committees they chair are slated to report, they say, "No report." You may be relieved, because you can go home sooner! Yet when the chairperson of the service committee says, "No report," are we not puzzled? Should any church, for example, ever fail to have a report on serving the poor and needy?

Give us a break—the world is falling apart.

And what about members who attend meetings infrequently? At their installation did they mean it when they said they would attend *faithfully*?

Now I know that we differ widely in our basic personalities—the Myers Briggs Type Indicator posits sixteen different types. By nature some of us are simply more structured than others. Moreover, some effective leaders throughout church history would have to plead guilty to the above charges.

Yet God is faithful and wants us to be faithful. God kept the covenants God made with the children of Israel. And the psalmist says in this psalm that God made a covenant with David to establish David's descendants forever. The psalmist was overwhelmed with God's faithfulness. He sings of it, he proclaims it.

We too proclaim it and sing of it: "Great is Thy faithfulness! Morning by morning new mercies I see; All I have needed Thy hand hath provided; Great is Thy faithfulness, Lord, unto me!"[16] Look at the basis for this great hymn in Lamentations 3:22, 23.

Yes, the Lord we worship is faithful. We could not go on without God's new mercies every morning. Thus how can we *not* be faithful to God and one another?

The Misuse of Power

"Set Uriah in the forefront of the hardest fighting, and then draw back from him, so that he may be struck down and die" (2 Sam. 11:15). Read 2 Samuel 11: 14–27.

C an you believe it? How could David, the man after God's own heart, commit adultery with the wife of one of his soldiers and then arrange to have him killed? Is it not one of the most flagrant abuses of power in the Bible?

"But wait a minute," you say. "David's terrible deed has absolutely no relevance for our church work."

Though I wish it didn't, I fear it does. Perhaps our misuse of power does pale in comparison to what David did. And surely it's subtler. Yet we still misuse power. To win our little church battles, we manipulate circumstances and people like pawns on a chessboard.

Still not convinced? Instead of using their power to achieve *God's* purposes, church boards may use their power to achieve *their* purposes. Clergy may stack the deck in a vote facing the board. Staff members may secretly maneuver to undermine another staff member. We may try to block a certain person we don't like from being nominated to a leadership position. Anyone can cleverly use parliamentary procedure to cut off debate on an issue. Don't our actions often prove we believe the end justifies whatever means we use? Don't we assume we know what's best for the church?

The issue here is not to do away with power! Power can and should be used to accomplish God's will. Only let's make sure we want to accomplish God's will and do it without employing highly questionable methods.

When we search our hearts, we discover dark corners lurking there. But remember David. Even adultery and "malice murder" were not enough to cut him off from God's forgiveness. We too can be forgiven by the One who came in the line of David and who, when crucified, was called "the power of God and the wisdom of God" (1 Cor. 1:24b).

Jesus, you see, forever transformed our understanding of power. *Real power kneels and washes feet. And real power loves all the way to the cross so that we who abuse power can be forgiven.* Now that's a powerful thought.

Slow to Anger

> "...let everyone be quick to listen, slow to speak, slow to anger; for your anger does not produce God's righteousness" (James 1:19b–20). *Read James 1:19–21.*

T hink back over all the meetings you've ever attended. Depending on your age, you may come up with a short list or a very long list. Either way, most of us say we attend far too many meetings!

Now think about the meetings in which people exploded in anger. Also recall the times when you blew up. Did others react in anger too? And did you feel remorseful the next day, saying to yourself, "Wish I had held my tongue"?

I like what James says: "Let everyone be *quick* to listen, *slow* to speak, *slow* to anger." But what usually happens? We are *slow* to listen, *quick* to speak, and *quick* to anger. Haven't we got it backward?

No wonder anger often has a destructive effect on meetings. Normally, exploding at people "does not produce God's righteousness," which is acting as God wants us to act.

Here's our problem in a nutshell: We don't know how to process anger. Rather, we vent it or suppress it, as David R. Mace says.[17] Venting anger, while justified in the face of great evil, may only create more anger. *Suppressing* anger, while sometimes wise in delicate situations, still drives it underground where it can cause us to do a slow burn. *Processing* anger, on the other hand, requires us to express it but in nonthreatening ways. "I feel angry when we keep going around in circles on this issue." Thus we acknowledge what is going on in *us* without attacking *others*. We therefore enable others to work on the issue with us, because they don't feel threatened.

The good news is that we can become angry without sinning. "Be angry but do not sin; do not let the sun go down on your anger" (Eph. 4:26). If you become angry, do not let the sun go down on your anger; in other words, express it soon, not later in the church parking lot! *But remember how to process it.*

And what about adopting the following rule in your meetings: "When we become angry, we'll describe our anger without attacking others"? Might be worth a try.

When Jealousy Rears its Ugly Head

"For he realized that it was out of jealousy that the chief priests had handed him over" (Mark 15:10). *Read Mark 15:6–15.*

Give Pontius Pilate some credit, for this tragic figure could read earthly motives. Did the religious authorities hand over Jesus because they were jealous of him? Perhaps. If so, of what were they jealous? His popularity with the people? Because he spoke as one having authority? His power to heal? His undeniable character, presence, and being? Maybe Pilate wasn't entirely right, but surely jealousy was a powerful, driving motive behind their action.

Jealousy is an old, old story. As old as Cain who murdered his brother Abel. As old as Joseph's brothers who threw him into a pit and left him with no water. As old as Saul hurling a spear at David after the women danced and sang, "Saul has killed his thousands, and David his ten thousands" (1 Sam. 18:7).

And sooner or later jealousy invades every church staff, every board, and every committee. Are you really happy when someone always speaks the right word at the right time? Are you ready to dance in the streets when someone else gets credit for an idea you *thought* but didn't *share* with the group?

Yes, we often wear the face of jealousy. We betray ourselves in a thousand ways, from a faint smile to the inflection in our voices. And we may even rejoice when those we have envied suffer a misfortune—a horrible thought.

Any hope for us? Of course. The One who was delivered up *out of* jealousy now delivers us *from* jealousy. A crucified Lord looks forgivingly upon us when speak a negative word about a coworker while others are praising her. And he looks forgivingly upon us every time we work to keep others from receiving acclaim.

There's even more good news. The Lord who forgives also pours love "into our hearts through the Holy Spirit..." (Rom. 5:5). With the Spirit's help we begin to move toward those of whom we are jealous. We assess why they enjoy the acclaim we want. And we also realize and value of the gifts God has given us.

Without a doubt jealousy is potent. But in the final analysis it's no match for the transforming power of God's love. Accept it!

Dealing with Difficult People

"Zacchaeus, hurry and come down; for I must stay at your house today" (Luke 19:5). *Read Luke 19:1–10.*

Nothing so vexes us as dealing with difficult people. Sometimes they talk too much. Or they may have an irritating personality. Or they may take theological positions we don't like. Or they may espouse values we abhor. Or they may be negative people. Or...you fill in the blanks, because you know exactly what I mean. You work with such people, you live with them, and you worship with them.

How do you act toward those people you don't like? with silence? with avoidance? with confrontation? I'll bet that neither strategy helped you or them. Usually, the way we act toward such people makes them worse, drives them deeper into their patterns of irritation and negativity.

Look at poor Zacchaeus, for example. For starters, he collected *taxes*. Enough said? But not only that, he collected taxes for the hated Romans, their foreign dominators. Moreover, he had grown rich at their expense. No wonder the townspeople despised Zacchaeus! Nor should we wonder why he had to climb a sycamore tree to see Jesus when he passed by. Wouldn't the people take great delight in keeping this short man from seeing over their heads?

So imagine their shock—disgust?—when Jesus said, "Zacchaeus, hurry and come down; for I must stay at your house today." They began to grumble, because Jesus had gone in to be the guest of a man whom they regarded as a sinner. But Jesus loved the unlovely, the irritating, the despised. And his love made them come alive. To Jesus Zacchaeus was a person to be loved, not a plague to be avoided.

Certainly the love of Jesus dramatically changed Zacchaeus. He decided to give half of his possessions to the poor and offered to pay back anyone he had defrauded fourfold, far more than the law required. In fact, Jesus declared that salvation had come to the house of Zacchaeus, because he too was a son of Abraham.

Now think again about those people you work with in your church. Is it possible that underneath their irritating behavior lies a new person waiting to bloom? But it won't happen if you keep avoiding or stonewalling them. Instead, look for ways to relate, ideas to endorse, and qualities to praise. You might discover another Zacchaeus or two!

Are You a Workaholic?

"Be still, and know that I am God" (Ps. 46:10).

In a way, it's strange that I would write a devotional on workaholics. My family members and friends might be inclined to jest, "It takes one to spot one!" For they know that I have worked hard all my life—too hard, some would say. Perhaps I'm still in denial, but I'm only a borderline workaholic who by the grace of God is learning to relax and enjoy more of the good gifts God has given me.

But why this topic for church leaders? Simply because I believe workaholism is a real problem for many church leaders. Don't some ministers in moments of honesty tell you they are married to the church? Don't other staff members often say the same? And what about board members and other leaders? They too may be inflicted with this disease that relentlessly drives us day and night to work, work, work until we fall into the grave.

One irony about workaholism is its power to impress people, even to draw rave reviews. "She's the hardest working minister I have ever seen." "What a church leader! He's here every time the doors open." "If you need someone to do a job around here, ask her. She's extremely busy, but she'll work it in somehow." It even appears that workaholism is the only addiction that elicits a favorable response.

But we pay a price for workaholism. As in any addiction, we cry out with Paul, "I do not understand my own actions" (Rom. 7:15a). We see that we are driven to work all of our waking hours. Even on holidays and days off we sneak in a little work. I know. I've been there and done that! (More often than I like to admit.)

From the heart of the gospel comes a freeing word: God loves us as we are. We can never preach enough sermons, or chair enough committees, or teach enough classes to put ourselves over with God. In God's love we can relax and realize that God is in control.

Already I can sense your resistance. Are you saying, "But don't you want people to work hard? We've got enough slackers as it is."

Yes, but God does not ask us to work so compulsively that we become exclusively absorbed in the church or anything else. Don't we all need to remember these words: "Be still, and know that I am God"? *After all, how can we really serve God if we don't know who God is?*

And the Walls Came Tumblin' Down

*"There is no longer Jew or Greek, there is no longer
slave or free, there is no longer male and female; for all
of you are one in Christ Jesus" (Gal. 3:28). Read
Galatians 3:23–29.*

Thank God for the revolutionary gospel of Jesus
Christ. The wall between Jew and Greek tumbled
down first; then the wall between slave and free. And
finally the wall between male and female came tumblin'
down.

In my lifetime I have witnessed a revolution in church
leadership. Gone are the days when women exercised
power and influence only in the home, Sunday school, and
women's organizations. We have entered a new era in which
women now serve on most church boards, in the pulpit,
and even predominate as candidates in some theological
seminaries. Truly, women have come a long way in the
church, as well as everywhere else in society.

And the changing landscape in church leadership has
been overwhelmingly good for the church. After working
with women increasingly in church and seminary for my
entire career, I rejoice in their unique gifts, like nurture and
support, that they bring to leadership. I marvel at how
many women lead from a relational, collaborative, and
empowering paradigm. I appreciate the diligence with
which many women address the work of the church.

Not that we haven't had problems to work out and adjustments to make. Some men still work from a more hierarchical perspective and attempt to assert their power. Women may resent being put exclusively into nurturing and supportive roles in staff relations. They may also be suspicious of some of us men when we are tempted to use images of service and servanthood to keep them in subservient roles. And clearly the closer working relationships between men and women have heightened the potential for romantic interests to develop—in some cases with disastrous results.

But on balance, women in leadership positions have enormously enriched the church. In no way can we or should we turn back the clock to the time when women were not heard in our church councils, or in our pulpits either. As our text says, we are all one in Christ Jesus.

Thus, as you begin your meeting or reflect on your church life today, thank *God* for your women leaders. And thank *them* too!

The Greatest

"A dispute also arose among them as to which one of them was to be regarded as the greatest" (Luke 22:24). Read Luke 22:24–27.

W as it not inevitable that the disciples would argue about which one of them was the greatest? After all, this argument goes on everyday among us in all walks of life. A former boxer even called himself "The Greatest!" (And I'll have to admit that he was.) A marvelous quarterback declared that he was on track to become the greatest to ever play football.

Need other examples? A baseball player is miffed because he no longer is the highest paid player in the sport. A CEO, making millions, is disgruntled because the stockholders want to put the brakes on his compensation. A successful football coach is disappointed because he has never won the Super Bowl.

Unquestionably, church life is no exception. Ministers long for tall-steepled churches. Leaders push hard for their agendas at board meetings and want to chair only the most important committees. More than once I myself have wondered about my place in God's scheme of things. Haven't you?

Now we may not openly argue among ourselves about who is the greatest. We are far too sophisticated to do that.

After all, we have read the gospel. We know how unbecoming it was for the disciples so to argue. And we usually don't like people with big egos. Still, do we not secretly wonder about our place in the kingdom?

As always, Jesus gives us a reality check. Only his understanding of reality is based on life in the kingdom of God, not the world. If you want to be great in the kingdom, Jesus says, become like the youngest. And if you want to lead, you must serve—even wait tables.

Thus Jesus stuns us as much as the disciples. That's not how we wanted the dispute about the greatest to be resolved. We wanted (expected?) Jesus to declare us the winner!

So, sobered by the gospel, we return to our church work. We listen with more acceptance to one another before we speak. We affirm others. We admit our faults. And we work together for mutually satisfying solutions to our conflicts. But why? Because we can't get out of our minds and hearts the haunting figure of him who said, *"But I am among you as one who serves"* (Luke 22:27b).

Appendix

Discussion Questions for Each Devotional

Part 1—Foundations of Christian Leadership

Called by God

1. What can we do to put ourselves in a position to hear God's call to us?

2. Discuss the various ways God calls us—to be disciples of Christ, in our jobs, and in our service to the church. Which call is basic?

3. As you respond to God's call, in what sense do you travel alone? In what sense do you need companions along the way?

Chosen to Serve

1. When did you first become aware that Jesus was calling you to serve him?

2. What was your first leadership position in the church? How were you recruited for the job?

3. What was the best training the church ever gave you for a job?

Rooted and Built Up in Christ

1. What new teachings particularly threaten the Christian faith in your context?

2. What is the proper attitude for Christians when confronted by teachings such as New Age philosophy?

3. How can Christians ensure that they will continue to be grounded in Christ?

Empowered by the Spirit

1. What criteria do you most often follow when choosing leaders for your church?

2. To what extent is your church influenced by the criterion of choosing leaders to serve who are full of the Holy Spirit?

3. What are the characteristics of someone who is empowered by the Spirit?

Connected with the Body of Christ

1. In what sense is it good to be an individualist? How can it be bad?

2. How would your church work improve if all your members took seriously their membership in the body of Christ?

3. How do you presently feel most connected with the body of Christ?

Enriched by Fellowship

1. What are the greatest sources of fellowship in your church?

2. How are divine and human fellowship related?

3. What can you do in your board or committee or other church group to deepen fellowship with God and one another?

Surrounded by Witnesses

1. Which biblical heroes and heroines have most inspired you? How?

2. What denominational heroes and heroines have been most inspiring to you?

3. Name and describe some of the Christians you have known whose faith has been inspirational for you.

Devoted to Prayer

1. What is your group's practice in regard to prayer?

2. Do you routinely agree to pray for one another until you meet again?

3. What would you need to do to pray more faithfully and effectively in your meetings?

Guided by Scripture

1. Discuss the various viewpoints in your group about what it means to say the Bible is inspired by God.

2. How does your group use scripture in its work?

3. What do you need to do in your personal life to receive greater benefit from scripture?

Motivated by Love

1. Why do you think that loving God with your whole being is the greatest commandment?

2. What does it mean to love your neighbor as yourself?

3. Discuss why these love commandments give your life meaning and purpose.

Focused on the Kingdom of God

1. Discuss the characteristics of the most faithful and effective Christian leaders you have known.

2. Someone has said that many church leaders put their jobs first, their families second, their hobbies third, and the church fourth in their order of priorities. Do you agree? What are your priorities?

3. Why is it essential for Christian leaders to focus on the kingdom of God as their first priority?

Endowed with Faith

1. Discuss what it means to have faith in Jesus as Son of God, as Lord, and as Savior.

2. When your church selects leaders, is faith in Jesus Christ one of the essential criteria by which persons are chosen?

3. What would you do if someone left your church $100,000 in a will? How does faith in Jesus Christ affect your answer?

Urged on by Christ's Love

1. What to you is the most amazing thing about the love of Christ?

2. Discuss how Christ's love has kept you steady in difficult days.

3. In what ways are you reflecting the love of Christ in the way you are working with others?

Part 2—Characteristics of Christian Leaders

Doers of the Word

1. Discuss how the downfall of national Christian leaders has hurt the public perception of the Christian faith.

2. Does God require a higher standard for church leaders than for rank-and-file members? Defend your answer.

3. What is the most difficult aspect of the Christian faith for you personally?

Forgive Each Other!

1. Reflect on times in your life when you have been forgiven and cite examples.

2. Why is it so hard to forgive?

3. How could the power of forgiveness help your group right now?

The Good News about Jesus

1. Is witnessing easy or hard for you? Explain.

2. From whom did you learn the gospel? What was he or she like?

3. Discuss the difference between having a *gift* for evangelism and having a *role* in evangelism.

Overcoming Evil with Good

1. How do you stop the all too human tendency to retaliate against those who wrong you?

2. Discuss how Jesus overcame evil with good in his own life.

3. In what ways does your church presently need to overcome evil with good in your community?

In Whom There is No Deceit

1. What biblical examples of deceit do you recall that reveal the destructiveness of deceit?

2. Why is deceit a poison pill that destroys human relationships?

3. Describe someone you know who is deeply sincere and reflect on how his or her sincerity affects you.

The Joy that Christ Gives

1. How is the joy that Christ gives different from how the world thinks of joy?

2. When you remember Christ, what picture comes to mind—joy or sorrow, or both? Discuss.

3. Why do you think it's so difficult to find people who have the joy of Jesus down in their hearts?

The Peace of Christ

1. What to you is the most unusual thing about how Christ died?

2. What do most people you know think about when they say they want peace?

3. Can you receive peace by pursuing it directly, or does it come as a by-product? Explain.

The Conviction of Things Not Seen

1. Recall examples of how you launched out in faith and discovered that God was guiding you at every step.

2. Discuss occasions when your church was sorely tested in believing that enough volunteers or money would be forthcoming to enable a program or even the church to survive.

3. What resources of the Christian faith help keep your faith strong?

Hope That Does Not Disappoint

1. What examples of hopelessness do you see in our society, particularly in your community?

2. Do you think it's essential to believe in life after death to have hope in this life?

3. When you are most discouraged, how does the Christian faith restore your hope?

Diligent or Lackadaisical?

1. Discuss how diligence can improve both morale and concern for mission in the church.

2. How can you enable your leaders to become more diligent in their work?

3. Consider how the diligence of leaders affects those with whom they work.

Mature, Yet Immature

1. Review why an awareness of immaturity is actually a mark of maturity.

2. What does your denomination teach about the possibility of achieving a state of perfection in this life?

3. Discuss Paul's goal of Christian maturity, which is knowing Christ, sharing in his sufferings, and inheriting eternal life. How does this goal differ from many of our human goals?

A Leader is...Trustworthy

1. Discuss the importance of trust in any relationship.

2. What do you think would happen if our present generation fails to transmit the Christian faith to the next generation? Could Christianity later reappear?

3. Someone once said that to be trusted is a greater compliment than to be loved. In what sense is this true?

Faith, Hope, Love: And the Winner Is...

1. Substitute your name in 1 Corinthians 13:4–7 and discuss the results.

2. Which characteristic of love in Paul's hymn to love is most difficult for you?

3. Why did Paul say that love was the greatest of faith, hope, and love?

Part 3—Christian Leadership Skills

God's Servants, Working Together

1. Share illustrations of how collaboration has worked in your church or business or community.

2. Why is it so difficult to collaborate with others in solving problems?

3. Discuss the similarities between our understanding of collaboration and the biblical image of the church as the body of Christ in 1 Corinthians 12.

Sober Judgment

1. How applicable are Bill Marriott's six keys to better relationships to church work?

2. Are there differences between male and female leaders in the way we think of ourselves when we lead?

3. How does Paul's concept of the church as a body facilitate working relationships in the church?

Learning to Delegate

1. Why are so many people reluctant to delegate responsibility to others?

2. Discuss the advantages of delegation both for leaders and followers.

3. Share personal examples of how delegation improved working relationships in your church.

Listen to Me!

1. What are the greatest impediments to good listening?

2. Let the leader whisper something privately to the person next to him or her and ask them to do the same thing. When all have finished, compare the first statement with the last.

3. What are the effects of careful listening upon you?

Bearing Burdens

1. How can you do a better job in your group of discovering and bearing the burdens of others?

2. Discuss the difficulty of bearing others' burdens without assuming responsibility for their lives.

3. Folk wisdom declares, God doesn't place on you more than you can bear. Do you agree or disagree?

The Encourager

1. Share examples of how a word of encouragement has helped you.

2. Discuss the difference between encouragement and false assurance.

3. How can you encourage others without necessarily condoning everything they do?

Expecting Excellence

1. Name two Christian leaders you have most admired. What were they like?

2. Discuss how you recruit people to fill both elected and volunteer positions in your church.

3. In your recruiting do you stress the need for excellence in the job?

Where There is No Vision

1. In your church do you create a climate in which people can share their visions for the church?

2. Discuss instances of how church leaders have virtually imposed ill-conceived visions on their members.

3. Name occasions when churches conceived compelling visions for the future and energized you.

From Vision to Mission

1. When members share their vision for your church, how do people characteristically respond?

2. What is the proper response to make to shared visions?

3. How should you test the validity of a vision?

Decisions, Decisions!

1. Track the process by which you made a recent decision in your church. Did you consult members? Were they truly heard?

2. Discuss a decision your church made that created dissension. Was the *way* in which the decision was made a factor?

3. How may this discussion of the decision-making process in your church affect various decisions you face now?

Gathering Input to Discern God's Will

1. How much importance do you attach to seeking the input of the Holy Spirit in your deliberations?

2. Have you ever had any formal training in how to be a more effective group member? Would such training help?

3. Explain how you can be open and receptive to the ideas of others without necessarily agreeing with them.

Reconciliation: Ministry and Gift

1. Review the difference between reconciliation as *our* ministry and *God's* gift.

2. In a conflict what can you do to create a climate in which reconciliation can take place?

3. It has been said that reconciliation cannot happen *through* you unless it happens *to* you. Do you agree? If so, why?

Abused but Not Abusive

1. What effects does a loving and forgiving response have on those who inflict pain on others? Discuss.

2. Evaluate Stephen Covey's statement: It's not what happens to us, but our response to what happens to us that hurts us.

3. What are the enemies facing your church now? How can you respond positively to those situations and conditions?

Part 4—Issues for Christian Leaders

No Conflict in the Church?

1. How does your church usually handle conflict?

2. Describe a conflict in your church that has been resolved with quite positive benefits. What can you learn from that conflict resolution?

3. Why do we especially fear conflict in the church?

The Church: A Body, A System

1. Does thinking of the church as a system shed any light on recent conflicts in your church?

2. Recall incidents in your church when a seemingly trivial matter touched off a chain reaction of consequences.

3. How can the systems theory help you the next time you undertake changing a program in your church?

Do It My Way!

1. What is the effect of constant overcontrolling on any group? on you personally?

2. Discuss the merits of using the suggested questions in the text on a regular basis in your group.

3. How can you receive greater input from the members of your group?

Love is Not Touchy

1. Discuss when touchiness might be a sin.

2. How does your group or church typically handle touchy people? Does that approach work?

3. How can you be both sensitive to the feelings of people, yet concerned about the work of the church at the same time?

Tending the Flock of God

1. Why is the church so often willing to tolerate incompetence?

2. Why is the attitude you take toward your work so crucial in the church?

3. Discuss ways to improve both your competence and your attitude in your work together.

God's Faithfulness and Ours

1. Discuss how our faithfulness is rooted in God's faithfulness to us.

2. How can you hold one another more accountable in your work and thereby encourage faithfulness?

3. Someone once said that it was a greater compliment to be trusted than to be loved. Do you agree?

The Misuse of Power

1. Power corrupts and absolute power corrupts absolutely, it has been said. Do you agree or disagree?

2. Discuss the subtle ways power is commonly misused.

3. How can you best ensure that you use power for good?

Slow to Anger

1. Recall and share events when you have suppressed anger instead of processing it.

2. Why do we fear anger so much?

3. Discuss how you in your church or group can best process anger. Would it help to establish ground rules?

When Jealousy Rears its Ugly Head

1. Why do you think the chief priests were so jealous of Jesus? Was Pilate right in assuming that it was out of jealousy that the chief priests delivered Jesus up?

2. It has been said that jealousy is a sin that particularly besets church leaders, especially clergy. Do you agree?

3. How does the gospel help us deal with jealousy?

Dealing with Difficult People

1. Talk about the difference between caring for people and opposing their unacceptable behavior.

2. Give other examples from the gospel about how Jesus loved the unlovely.

3. What is the gospel's greatest incentive for us to love difficult and unlovely people?

Are You a Workaholic?

1. Why do we tend to joke about workaholism but take seriously other forms of addiction? Do you think that workaholism is really an addiction?

2. How does your church encourage workaholism?

3. As you lead the work of your church, do you encourage people to be still and know that God is God? How?

And the Walls Came Tumblin' Down

1. Review briefly changing leadership patterns in your church for the last twenty-five years. How has the role of women changed?

2. Discuss the positive side of having women serve at every level in the church.

3. Do you think that, generally speaking, women lead from a more relational, collaborative paradigm while men lead from a more competitive, hierarchical paradigm? Illustrate your answer.

The Greatest

1. How does the American concept of success further fuel the desire to be great today?

2. Who were the truly great people you have known in your church life, and why were they great?

3. How can your church continue to encourage you to be servant-leaders?

Notes

[1] See Donald E. Messer, *Contemporary Images of Christian Ministry* (Nashville: Abingdon, 1989), 127.

[2] "Blest Be the Tie That Binds," *The Presbyterian Hymnal* (Louisville: Westminster/John Knox Press, 1990), no. 438.

[3] H. Richard Niebuhr, *The Purpose of the Church and Its Ministry* (New York: Harper & Row, 1956), 27.

[4] *Church Officer Pre-Ordination Curriculum Leaders Guide* (Philadelphia: The Geneva Press, 1975), 11.

[5] *The American Heritage Dictionary of the English Language* (New York: Dell, 1970), 201.

[6] Bill Marriott, "Keys to Better Relationships," *Bottom Line Personal* (January 1,1997), 14.

[7] Samuel V. Wilson, quoted in *Campaign News* (Winter 1997), 2. This was an occasional publication for "To Sustain the Mission," a financial campaign of Hampden-Sydney College, Hampden-Sydney, VA 23943.

[8] See Alvin J. Lindgren and Norman Shawchuck, *Let My People Go* (Nashville: Abingdon, 1980), 51–78. These pages provide a helpful discussion of decision making and informed my devotional.

[9] Speed B. Leas, *Moving Your Church through Conflict* (Washington, D.C.: The Alban Institute, 1985), 9.

[10] Stephen R. Covey, *The 7 Habits of Highly Effective People* (New York: Simon & Schuster, 1989), 73.

[11] See Viktor E. Frankl, *Man's Search for Meaning* (New York: Washington Square, 1967).

[12] See Kenneth R. Mitchell, *Multiple Staff Ministries* (Philadelphia: Westminster Press, 1988), 32–42. Mitchell discusses many principles about systems in these pages, and I am here building primarily on his insights.

[13] See Edwin H. Friedman, *Generation to Generation: Family Process in Church and Synagogue* (New York: Guilford Press, 1985), 193–219.

[14] Speed B. Leas, "Can colleagues co-league on a church staff?" *Action Information*, n.d., 5.

[15] Ibid.

[16] "Great Is Thy Faithfulness," *The Presbyterian Hymnal*, no. 276.

[17] See David R. Mace, *Close Companions: The Marriage Enrichment Handbook* (New York: Continuum, 1982), 90–99. On page 98, Mace also discusses a fourth way of dealing with anger: *dissolving* it, as when you quickly realize you misunderstood a comment made by your spouse. Your body tension relaxes and you are soon back to normal.

Bibliography

Callahan, Kennon L. *Effective Church Leadership: Building on the Twelve Keys.* San Francisco: Harper & Row, 1990.

_____. *Twelve Keys to an Effective Church.* San Francisco: Harper & Row, 1990.

Carroll, Jackson W. *As One With Authority: Reflective Leadership in Ministry.* Louisville, Ky.: Westminster/John Knox Press, 1991.

Cosgrove, Charles H., and Dennis D. Hatfield. *Church Conflict: The Hidden Systems Behind the Fights.* Nashville: Abingdon Press, 1994.

Covey, Stephen R. *The 7 Habits of Highly Effective People.* New York: Simon & Schuster, 1989.

Friedman, Edwin H. *Generation to Generation: Family Process in Church and Synagogue.* New York: Guilford Press, 1985.

Greenleaf, Robert K. *Servant Leadership.* New York: Paulist Press, 1977.

Hahn, Celia Allison. *Growing in Authority, Relinquishing Control.* Washington, D.C.: The Alban Institute, 1994.

Halverstadt, Hugh F. *Managing Church Conflict.* Louisville, Ky.: Westminster/John Knox Press, 1991.

Hopewell, James F. *Congregation: Stories and Structure.* Philadephia: Fortress Press, 1987.

Leadership Skills for Effective Ministry. Naperville, Ill.: Center for Parish Development, 1980.

Leas, Speed B. *Discover Your Conflict Management Style.* Washington, D.C.: Alban Institute,1984.

_____. *Moving Your Church Through Conflict.* Washington, D.C.: Alban Institute, 1985.

Lindgren, Alvin J., and Norman Shawchuck. *Let My People Go.* Nashville: Abingdon Press, 1980.

Likert, Rensis, and Jane Gibson Likert. *New Ways of Managing Conflict.* New York: McGraw-Hill, 1976.

Mead, Loren B. *The Once and Future Church.* Washington, D.C.: Alban Institute, 1991.

Messer, Donald E. *Contemporary Images of Christian Ministry.* Nashville: Abingdon Press, 1989.

Mitchell, Kenneth R. *Multiple Staff Ministries.* Philadelphia: Westminster Press, 1988.

Neuchterlein, Anne Marie. *Improving Your Multiple Staff Ministry*. Minneapolis: Augsburg, 1989.

Pappas, Anthony G. *Entering the World of the Small Church: A Guide for Leaders*. Washington, D.C.: Alban Institute, 1988.

Ramey, Robert H., Jr. *Growing Church Leaders: New Skills for New Tasks*. Decatur, Ga.: CTS Press, 1995.

Shawchuck, Norman, and Roger Heuser. *Leading the Congregation: Caring for Yourself While Serving the People*. Nashville: Abingdon Press, 1993.

A Systems Model of the Church in Ministry and Mission. Chicago: Center for Parish Development, n.d.